T0196065

SUPERNATURAL HEALING
EXISTS
DID YOU GET THE MEMO?

JACQUELYN D. GOLDEN, PH.D.

WESTBOW
PRESS®
A DIVISION OF THOMAS NELSON
& ZONDERVAN

WestBow Press books may be ordered through booksellers or by contacting:

WestBow Press
A Division of Thomas Nelson & Zondervan
1663 Liberty Drive
Bloomington, IN 47403
www.westbowpress.com
1 (866) 928-1240

Because of the dynamic nature of the Internet, any web addresses or links contained in this book may have changed since publication and may no longer be valid. The views expressed in this work are solely those of the author and do not necessarily reflect the views of the publisher, and the publisher hereby disclaims any responsibility for them.

Any people depicted in stock imagery provided by Thinkstock are models, and such images are being used for illustrative purposes only. Certain stock imagery © Thinkstock.

Scripture taken from the King James Version Bible.

Scripture quotations are from the ESV® Bible (The Holy Bible, English Standard Version®), copyright © 2001 by Crossway, a publishing ministry of Good News Publishers. Used by permission. All rights reserved.

ISBN: 978-1-9736-0568-3 (sc)
ISBN: 978-1-9736-0569-0 (hc)
ISBN: 978-1-9736-0567-6 (e)

Library of Congress Control Number: 2017915145

Print information available on the last page.

WestBow Press rev. date: 11/20/2017

This book is written
in memory of my dear friend,

~ Dorothy J. McIntosh~

You showed me
what unconditional love
looks like in word and deed.

I'll never forget
what you did for my sister and me
when we did not even realize
we had a need.

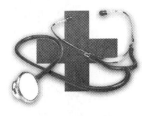

ACKNOWLEDGMENTS

Thank-you seems so small when I think of how you gave of your support, resources, knowledge, skills, time, and enthusiasm to fan the flame for writing this book thus keeping it burning and alive in me. Your contributions fueled my desire to bring this book to life and encouraged me not to abandon the task. So, here's a big – **THANK YOU!!!!!!!**

I salute and esteem you highly:

Perry Alford, Jr. (Photographer) – While posing for pictures is not something I particularly care to do, you created an atmosphere that kept me smiling – thanks for capturing those moments!

Christopher Coleman (Book Project Consultant) – I can rely on you to give legs to an idea and bring it to life! I love the way you make things happen.

Deshon Gales (Cover Art Designer) – Your mastery in how you visually bring concepts to life stopped me in my tracks upon first glance of your work! You have exceptional skill, and I thank you for sharing it with me.

Vincent F. A. Golphin, Editor (The Book Doctor) – You are simply the best at helping individuals tell their "own" stories!

Brian Henry (Photographer) – Being a part of your expression via photography stirred up the artist in me – thanks for capturing those moments and for reminding me that I possess another talent that I should resurrect!

Barbara Peterson (Proofreader) – You are my extra pair of eyes! Thank you for your eagle-eye precision vision and seeing what I could not see. I hope to see you in the next round.

Jan Buckner Walker (Cruciverbalist) –You've been my biggest supporter since the first day I met you, and that's been a long, long time ago. Thank you for believing in me!

CONTENTS

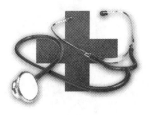

FOREWORD

I have known Jackie since she was a little girl. I had the privilege to pastor her father, the late Rev. Howard Golden, Sr. and mother, Mother Christine Golden, both who were faithful to the Lord's work and given to prayer.

Jackie is her parents' legacy. This determined, bright and educated young woman reminds us in this book that there are two reports, man's report and the report of the Lord. Jackie shares rich testimonies of how steadfast prayer and standing on the word of God reversed negative reports and brought about supernatural healing in her life. I pray that this book ignites the faith of the believer and causes others to want to know about the God of the Bible.

Well done, Jackie!

Bishop Timothy T. Scott
Northern Mississippi Ecclesiastical Jurisdiction
Church of God in Christ, Inc.
Clarksdale, MS

A NOTE FROM THE EDITOR

"Open your mind," I said to myself as I began to edit this book, *Supernatural Healing Exists! Did You Get the Memo?*

I was not ready to dive into a narrative of vague claims with demands that the reader lay logic on the altar of belief. This book does not do that. Instead, Dr. Jacquelyn D. Golden shares a remarkable struggle against illness during which she experiences the depths of fear, sadness and depression, then finds herself lifted into hope on the shoulders of God.

Golden offers readers a "confession" in the classical Biblical form. The author tells about God's actions in her life and the actions of those God sends as an oration that begs readers to meditate on the Holy Spirit's power and the promises of the Holy Bible. In the relation of what He has done for her, and what God says He will do for humankind, the book reveals unheeded miracles that unfold every day.

People of faith will find inspiration in this work to rely even more on Divine Providence. Some might be moved to reconsideration and credit God's actions in their lives. Readers who have doubts or hesitations about the acceptance of healing miracles will find themselves curious about the ability of God to reach into human lives.

I am honored to have a role in the development of this work. May God bless the efforts of its author and those who have need of its message.

Vincent F. A. Golphin, Editor
The Book Doctor

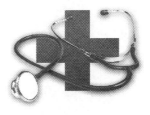

INTRODUCTION

Have you or a loved one ever been sick and wondered if God would heal your body? Did you pray for healing and nothing happened? Let me share this simple truth with you – God heals!

In this book, you will:

- Learn how you can overcome sickness and the fear that comes with it by default.
- Discover ways to combat doubt and unbelief in your healing journey.
- Master the three techniques to build and sustain your faith to the point of manifested promise, which are:
  - Believe God wants you well.
  - Program your mind and heart to receive (activate) healing in your body.
  - Stand in faith, and do not waiver.

I wrote this book because I want to see you well. I want to walk you through the process that worked for me as I struggled through the diagnosis and treatment of ovarian cysts, fibroids, and severe ulcerative colitis (UC), how pneumonia complicated my situation, and I almost died.

Each chapter is comprised of quick, easy-to-read topics. You will find a few facts, inspirational quotes and tips designed to aid you in your journey – things that you can immediately put into action.

Stay tuned to learn how I went from not being able to consume anything but a liquid diet for 12 days to today, when I eat whatever I want to eat and go wherever I want to go without any digestive issues. See how I thwarted The Enemy's plan to take me out prematurely!

Please, know that this book is not written to influence your decisions about seeking medical attention and taking prescription drugs. My goal is to urge you to include God in your health decisions and healing process.

Take a few minutes, and read Chapter 1 now!

Note: I make no claim to be a medical expert; I base my findings on Godly promise and experience.

Don't Panic – Pray!

As I walked through the door, my sister, Bonnie, stepped out of her normal greeting.

"What's wrong with you?" she said. "You look like you're pregnant!"

"Pregnant!" I silently screamed.

Bonnie saw me raise my right eyebrow. It was a look that resembled the stern but subtle glare my mother used to give from the choir stand if I talked to my friends as the pastor preached. The look warned that a good ole fashioned whipping would follow if she had to look again.

Whenever we got together, almost daily, Bonnie shared something funny about different customers throughout the day. She and her husband ran several businesses, among them a used furniture store. She would also tell short family stories, events that took place long before I was born. She was happily married, and I wasn't married at all.

Pregnant? I rolled the word through my mind again. I also heard a loud thump of dismay and felt disappointed. In a single moment, my sister who typically put a smile on my face had hurt me to the core. My heart sank.

How could a sibling whom I thought knew me best say that to me? I silently pondered. *How could she betray me?*

"Don't insult me like that," I said.

I *was* insulted. Bonnie knew my lifestyle. I was a go-getter in the pursuit of career, higher education, and God. All I did was work, take classes, and go to church. I lived by a righteous standard.

Pregnancy? Not possible.

Not only wasn't I married, but I did not engage in pre-marital sex, a fool-proof birth control method. Of all the people in my circle of family and friends, Bonnie should have known better. The risk of getting pregnant, or to rear a child alone, did not fit into my time-consumed lifestyle.

Monday through Friday, I worked as a personnel representative and taught classes for students enrolled in the elementary gifted education program in one of the New York State's public school systems. Tuesday and Thursday evenings, I taught computer classes in an adult education literacy program. On Saturdays, I taught computer literacy in the LeMoyne College Higher Education Preparation program. In addition, I was in a full-time Master's degree program, taught Sunday school, and served as a musician at my church.

Jackie Do Right

I felt utterly disgraced by what Bonnie asked because back then my career and almost every other daily activity were tied to rigid standards. I had rules for my spiritual life, too. They were carved in stone on the "Jackie-Do-Right" checklist. "Saved" girls did not allow guys to passionately kiss or touch them. And, by no means did you engage in premarital sex.

I governed my actions by mastering the church's *dos* and *dont's*, which I thought was paramount to building a relationship with Jesus, and that checklist was insulted by Bonnie's mere thought that I might be with child. My walk with Christ was rooted in unintentional ignorance at this time. Over time, my walk grew into a walk with Christ based on relationship and actions based on substantiated scripture, not just man's opinions.

I was part of a large crowd of believers in Jesus Christ that focused more on acts rather than relationship. A "do-right" list varied depending on your religious affiliation, and was passed down from generation to generation. All I desired was to do what pleased God – do what was right. If the church said a particular action pleased God and was right in His sight, I was on the track. If the church said a particular action was not pleasing in His sight, not doing it was my goal.

I was Pentecostal and affiliated with the Church of God in Christ. The "Jackie-Do-Right" checklist consisted of a roll of restrictions. In some circles, women were forbidden to cut or dye their hair. In addition to accepting Jesus as Lord of your life, you were considered really "saved" if you did not wear pants, makeup or nail polish, open-toe shoes, dresses or tops with no sleeves, tight or fitted dresses or skirts that fall above the knees. Other general restrictions included not playing sports, and especially not on Sundays. Movies, "ungodly" music, smoking, and alcohol were also forbidden.

Fortunately, I learned over time that living solely by this checklist of rules was not necessarily living in Christ. That checklist simply created boundaries for me and motivated me to search out reasons for the things people would say, "don't do," but could not explain. "Grandma did or didn't do it, so it must be right or it must be wrong" determined the behavior of many of my family and friends, like an old wives' tale I heard down through the years:

> "A man's wife sent him to the store for a ham. After he bought it, she asked him why he didn't have the butcher cut off the end of the ham. 'This old boy' asked his wife why she wanted the end cut off. She replied that her mother had always done it that way and that was reason enough for her. Since the wife's mother was visiting, they asked her why she always cut off the end of the ham. Mother replied that this was the way her mother did it; Mother, daughter, and 'this old boy' then decided to call Grandmother and solve this three-generation mystery. Grandmother promptly replied that she cut off the end of the ham because her roaster was too small to cook it in one piece."

In other accounts of this same story, many wives threw away the ends of the ham because they thought something was wrong with that part of the meat. The end of the ham was fine. The wrong was a surrender to unintentional ignorance.

Was it all for naught? No! My "Jackie-Do-Right" checklist taught me how to say no to temptation throughout life and to search for truth until I find it. So, I thank God for my "Jackie- Do-Right" checklist after all.

GOD'S ATTENTION-GETTER

While I was insulted by what Bonnie said, I later thanked her for being attuned to the minute details that concern me. The fact of the matter is that I'd become so busy, I did not see my body changing right before my eyes. I was 5' 9", weighed 130, and looked like I was three months pregnant but never noticed my bulging stomach because I was so busy. There was no abdominal or pelvic discomfort and no other physical signs to indicate something going on internally.

What I learned from this is that sometimes when people speak to you uncharacteristically, it is God's way of getting your attention. So, while I was upset with my sister, I acted on what she noticed. I called my doctor's office and talked to the nurse about what my sister had pointed out to me. The nurse conveyed this information to my doctor, who advised me to schedule a sonogram. She scheduled an appointment with my gynecologist for the upcoming week.

Appointment day arrived. I felt so alone as I awakened, even though I had a lot of family and friends at my disposal. Nevertheless, I mustered up enough strength to begin my fight for the day despite a fear of the unknown. The pre-examination requirements were that I not eat any food after midnight, so I could not make my normal breakfast run. To finish preparing for the appointment, I had to drink several ounces of water so that the technician and physician could get a good reading from the sonogram. I would have done anything to replace the water with a root beer, my drink of choice.

With extra time on my hands, I looked for ways to keep my mind in a good space. I filled the air with music and sang along. I pulled out my portable Yamaha keyboard and played along. To kill more time, I decided I would call my mother just to hear her voice. I knew this sound would give me the comfort I needed.

As the thought entered my mind, tears began to form in my eyes. I had to give myself a few minutes to pull myself together. Several minutes passed. I dialed Mom, and as I'd imagined, the lonely feeling that had crept in earlier began to fade away. Mom's voice put me at ease.

We had our usual conversation about what was going on in my home town, the weather, her sisters, and other family. Since I sometimes provided transportation for her sisters who lived near me in central New

York, she would insist that I share details of the time we spent together. Being around them was like watching *Saturday Night Live* without the profanity. It was the closest thing to her being with us. What an experience! As if she had initiated the call, Mom ended the call.

"Baby, I'm gonna let you go now," she said.

My tears began to form again. I quickly told her, "I love you, Mom, more than you'll ever know."

FACE TO FACE WITH FEAR

The hospital where I was to undergo the sonogram was about forty-five minutes from my apartment. Traffic worked in my favor. I arrived on time yet still in the stage of discovery. As I approached the intake desk, I felt weak in the knees. Tears started streaming down my face.

Instead of stating my name, I presented my driver's license because I simply could not speak. The intake specialist was a jewel. She stopped and directed her undivided attention to me. She walked from behind the desk to where I stood, offered me a drink, gave me the biggest smile, grabbed me by the hand, and whispered, "Everything's gonna be alright." The impact of her readiness to attend to me and her genuine sincerity gave me the strength I needed to pull myself together.

Now that I could speak, we were able to process my paperwork and get me ready for my examination. A few minutes later, my doctor's nurse came and led me to the examination room. Although the hallway that led to the examination room was not long, I felt like I was walking in slow motion, and it felt like a mile. We arrived finally, and the nurse instructed me to undress and put on a gown. I got settled into my gown and waited a short while for the doctor.

"How is your mother?" Dr. G. asked as he walked into the examination room. "How are your brothers and sisters?"

For some reason, the story about the 13 children of Howard and Christine Golden amazes everyone. "You know it's a lot of you guys," he said with a chuckle. That moment made the current situation easier to deal with, and with that, Dr. G. eased into the task at hand.

He reviewed his notes, which included the reasons for my concern.

I shared with him my recent encounter with my sister and how she said I looked pregnant.

"Are you sexually active?" he asked.

"No!" I replied emphatically with anger in my voice. The reply was firm. He looked startled.

"I don't mean to be offensive, but I have to ask these questions," he said. "Are you having any pain in your abdomen or stomach?"

"No, I feel fine," I replied more calmly.

"How are your menstrual cycles – are they on time? Do you bleed heavily?"

"All seems to be normal," I said.

"Very good," he said. "If you're ready, I'd like to begin the examination now."

It was the typical female examination that included both external and internal probing. In times past, I was always embarrassed by these types of tests. This time, being embarrassed really didn't matter because finding out what might be wrong with me was more important.

As Dr. G. completed the sonogram, I looked at the monitor and asked several questions like, "What does that circular formation represent?"

"I'll know more when we're done," he said.

I was about to ask the next question….

"Just relax, Jackie," he interjected. "I'll answer all your questions when I complete the exam and have had time to completely analyze my findings."

After about forty-five minutes, Dr. G. finished the examination and told me I was free to get dressed. He asked me to give him some time to write up his report. I gave him the thumbs-up on his request. He left the room, and I put on my clothes. It was about fifteen minutes later when Dr. G. returned with a concerned look on his face.

"That circular mass you asked me about is a cyst in your left ovary, and it is rather large," he said. "We need to remove it because we cannot risk this thing becoming ruptured. If it bursts, you could become very ill with infection. Worst-case scenario, I will need to remove your left ovary because it is attached to the cyst. And, there are fibroids in your uterus. We'll need to remove them as well, especially if you ever want to become pregnant."

WHERE IS GOD?

To help prepare me for the worst, Dr. G. gave me several pamphlets to read about fibroids and ovarian cysts and urged me to have the cyst removed immediately. Slow to leave me alone in the examination room, he said someone would be in very shortly to further discuss my options and assist in scheduling the surgery.

As he turned and left the room, I mentally fainted. For sure, I fainted in my spirit.

How can this be happening to me? I thought. *Did I do something wrong? Is God punishing me for something I have done or failed to do?*

Oh! How abandoned I felt.

Where is the great God I'd served for many years, I pondered while fighting tears.

I waited for Dr. G.'s assistant as I reviewed the pamphlets he gave me to learn more about these things that had invaded my body. The more I read, the more fearful I became. On the other hand, the more I read, the more I understood why my doctor communicated several options to me but strongly suggested he immediately remove the cyst.

I cannot recall that I had ever heard the terms "fibroid" or "cyst" before this time. Prior to this situation, I'd never been sick aside from having seasonal colds and allergy issues. I had never been hospitalized. If I had heard these terms, neither was something with which I had to deal. They really did not register in my mind and seemed rather foreign to me.

The pamphlets explained in more detail that if the cyst were to rupture and the fluid proved to be poisonous, it would rapidly infiltrate my body and could result in death. At the very least, infection would occur, and I'd be very sick and in severe pain. Antibiotics and other medications might not be able to combat the infection, either.

Dr. G.'s assistant arrived. "Hi, Jackie," she said skipping a lot of the formalities, which to me did not matter at this point. "I am here to discuss options for surgery with you and what that will entail if you decide to have it."

I needed to make a decision. I panicked at hearing my life could be in danger. I acted in the moment without readily bringing God into the situation. Since I had the best insurance available to me at that time, I instantly replied without hesitation, "Let's do this."

I panicked then prayed. In retrospect, I should have prayed first. If there were to be any panic, it would have had to come after the praying. Responding in the precise moment of receiving a diagnosis is key to sending a message to The Enemy (the devil) that your plan is to beat this attack. How you respond in the moment extends the life span of the momentum that is inherent in built-up prayer power and exercised faith.

We scheduled the surgery. When I got home, I reluctantly called my mother who at this time was about 70. I told her about the conversation I had with Bonnie, how I'd taken the next steps to see the doctor to find out if something was wrong inside my body, and finally dropped the bomb on her – I have to have surgery. To this day it amazes me how calmly she reacted. There was no panic in her voice. I was the one in panic.

What if the doctor cuts me open and damages a nerve or artery? I thought. *What if they give me too much anesthesia and I don't wake up? What if he determines that I need a hysterectomy? What if he removes my ovaries? What if I am unable to have children? Will a man want to marry me if I cannot? What if I die?"* These thoughts raced through my mind.

Always Count on Momma

Mom had medical issues of her own, but I knew that she would insist on coming to be by my side. To sway her from coming, I pretended to be strong and unafraid. But, you know how mothers do – they just know, do, and ask questions later.

Naturally, Mom was a strong-minded and fearless woman. She was determined in her pursuit of living life. She was an ambitious woman who had reared 13 children and went back to school and obtained her General Education Diploma (GED), and later became a Licensed Practical Nurse (LPN). Mom and I were in school at the same time!

It was with the same kind of ambition that she pursued the things of God. She was the kind of woman who not only nurtured her own children, but also mothered thousands. In fact, I have never witnessed her turning down anyone who came to her in need. If she had what you needed, she gave it. She was a God-fearing woman who believed He answered prayer. So, if prayer was all she had to give, she gave it.

Mom prayed for me, and her next words were, "Baby, Momma will be there." Now, to you this may be ordinary, but if you only knew the love that flowed through how my mother addressed her children and anyone with whom she would have real conversation, you'd understand better. "Baby" flowing from her lips was like having a heart massage. It was like tasting your favorite meal on your favorite holiday as you spent it with the people that are tied tightly to your heart, all packaged and gift wrapped into a single word. The next day she got on the Greyhound bus and headed my way.

After about twelve hours, the time for Mom's arrival was at hand. I got myself together and headed out to pick her up from the bus station. There she stood in her five-foot frame adorned with a big smile, love, and hope flowing from her directly into my soul. She reached out toward me and uttered these words: "Hey, Baby – Momma's here!" Upon laying eyes on her and hearing these words, the fear that had gripped and attempted to paralyze me went away almost instantly. Everything was going to be alright.

A few days passed by, and I underwent surgery. According to the doctor's report, there were no complications in removing the fibroids, and the cyst was removed just in time.

Ok, that's good, I thought to myself. *My life is now out of immediate danger.*

"But," he continued.

"But what?" I interrupted in a demanding tone.

"We had to remove your left ovary," he said.

In that moment, my future flashed before me at light speed. Sadness ushered me into depression in what seemed to be an instant. Scenarios played through my mind. I envisioned losing body parts in one scene. In another, I saw myself with a fifty percent chance of ever naturally giving birth to children. In a third, my mind fast forwarded to the question: What if the man I love and someday marry rejects me because of my inability to have children?

The "Why me?" question raced through my mind. Nothing would

shut it down. On the outside I looked normal. Inside, I was torn to pieces. I was not about to allow anyone see me cry, so I kept the tears packed down tightly. All I heard throughout life was that women are strong, and if you are a person of faith, you would not cry or be upset over a situation like this – all so far from the truth!

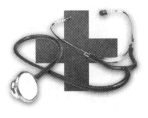

CHAPTER 2

Long Night of the Soul

The surgery was over. I gradually made steps back toward the life I once knew.

The physical wound was almost healed.

There was one scar that was nowhere near being healed – I was torn emotionally.

Often, I thought about the possibility of having to share my loss with a husband.

I would someday grow in love with someone. We would try to have a son. If successful and he agreed, we would name him Bryce Howard-Golden, plus whatever my husband's last name might be. I often thought about how my future spouse would react to seeing the scar on my body. Would he no longer be attracted to me? I stressed prematurely over things that I had not encountered – things that only time could ever reveal.

Instead of getting professional help to deal with those feelings, I became skillful at packing down the emotional pain. I carried a backpack of conflicted emotion and panic like a Sherpa up the mountain of my life. It was a long time before I learned how to move beyond the cross of Christ that reconnected me to God through forgiveness of sin, to relying on God to also take care of me in my daily life – good times, bad times, the hurt, and the worries.

THREE IN ME

Dad had passed away the year before I encountered the issue with the cyst, fibroids, and surgery. Mom's medical issues were getting worse.

My siblings were busy living their own lives. So, I didn't want to burden them with what I was feeling emotionally. Often, I found myself in tears when driving or home alone.

Crying was not the norm in our household. To make matters worse, I'd been told that strong believers don't waste time crying over things like what I'd gone through. They just pray. Time and experience taught me otherwise. When we express our emotions through tears, we can rest assured, as it says in Psalm 34:15, "The eyes of the Lord are upon the righteous, and his ears are open to their cry." Right, wrong, or indifferent, I had to rely on this passage. I cried many days but found strength in doing so.

I learned later that one third of who I was, was getting a good workout. We humans are tripartite:

- Each of us is a spirit.
- Each of our spirits lives in a body.
- We each possess a soul, which is the bedrock of our emotions.

Shedding tears is part of how we humans are created. Crying is OK!

According to Dr. Judith Orloff in her article, "The Health Benefits of Tears:"

> "Emotional tears have special health benefits. Crying makes us feel better, even when a problem persists. In addition to physical detoxification, emotional tears heal the heart. You don't want to hold tears back."

She states the findings of Dr. William Frey, biochemist and "tear expert" doctor at the Ramsey Medical Center in Minneapolis:

> "Dr. Frey discovered that reflex tears are 98% water, whereas emotional tears also contain stress hormones, which get excreted from the body through crying. After studying the composition of tears, Dr. Frey found that emotional tears shed these hormones and other toxins, which accumulate during stress. Additional studies

also suggest that crying stimulates the production of endorphins, our body's natural pain killer and 'feel-good' hormones."

My conclusion? Crying does the mind, body, and soul good.

I reflected on all that occurred, and thought, "What would have happened if I at the onset had fervently prayed for the fibroids and cyst to dissipate just like my fear did when Mom prayed for me?"

Had life-threatening danger truly been imminent?

Had there been enough time to give other less-invasive options a try?

Had there been time to give God a try?

To this day I wonder.

The years passed by, and to much dismay, I found myself in yet another battle with what I call the sister issue to cysts – fibroids. Here I go again!

SIDEBAR

Men should know that with some women, this condition can come with the territory. These are the situations that test the bonds of relationships and the levels of one's commitment to another person. When marriage vows say "in sickness and in health," these situations where illness creeps into the spaces between us and lead us to trying times are what those words are about. If you don't know women who have had this experience, try to relate to what you might want from someone if you were suddenly betrayed by your own body.

A SERIOUS SITUATION

Cysts are prevalent among African and Black American women. They seem to be rapidly expanding to other ethnic groups as well. "Each year, about 20,000 women in the United States get ovarian cancer," according to the Centers for Disease Control and Prevention (CDC). In 2010, in the United States, 19,959 women were diagnosed with ovarian cancer. In the same year, 14,572 women in the United States died from ovarian cancer.

"Among women in the United States, ovarian cancer is the eighth most common cancer and the fifth leading cause of cancer death, after lung and bronchus, breast, colorectal, and pancreatic cancers," the CDC states. "Ovarian cancer causes more deaths than any other cancer of the female reproductive system, but it accounts for only about 3% of all cancers in women. When ovarian cancer is found in its early stages, treatment is most effective."

The NIH Office of Research on Women's Health states, "Most American women will develop fibroids at some point in their lives. One study found that, by age 50, 70 percent of whites and 80 percent of African American women had fibroids." According to MIS for Women, "As many as 80% of African American women and 70% of Caucasian, Hispanic and Asian women develop uterine fibroids by the time they are 50."

I was a long way from age 50 the first time I battled fibroids. Years later when I was even older, I dealt with a second bout when I moved to Illinois. That relocation is discussed in Chapter 3, but here is what happened with that illness.

I tried a less-invasive option, Uterine Artery Embolization (UAE). UAE is a medical procedure in which an interventional radiologist uses a catheter to deliver small particles that block the blood supply to the uterine body. To my surprise, the fibroids began to shrink but at a rate that was slower than I desired. Somehow, I allowed an "I-want-it-now" spirit to creep in and drive my behavior. As if watching a microwave pop a bag of popcorn in a minute and thirty seconds, I wanted the fibroids to be gone rapidly. So, there I went again in early 2000…in the doctor's office examining the options, pro and con.

The fear that visited me during the cyst removal in the early 1990s was back. By this time, Mom had gone on to be in the presence of the Lord. The good news was that I remembered how she had prayed for me in the midst of my last crisis situation. I prayed, not focusing on the fear but rather very consciously denying fear the right to exist in the situation. I prayed in power and in the authority of the Name of Jesus. So, this time around I anchored myself in knowing that "God has not given us the spirit of fear; but of power, and of love, and of a sound mind" (2 Timothy 1:7).

The fear left!

When I had been confronted previously with the fibroids and cyst, I was caught off guard. Since that time, I had grown in my knowledge of the Word of God, His promises, and plan for my life. I spent countless hours in search of how I could get the results the Bible says I should get as a believer in Jesus Christ.

I was better equipped to deal with the challenge before me. However, I found myself shifting from relying on God's promise that I was already healed, and found myself relying on the strength of my great insurance plan to deliver me.

Do you see how easy it is to slip in and out of enforcing the power of God's Word and promises?

I had the fibroids surgically removed. Like the first surgery, this one was successful, but this time I did not lose anything else in my body. Thank God!

Second Thoughts

Even now, I wonder what might have happened had I prayed in faith in the moment of diagnosis, commanded the abnormal growths to leave my body, and then waited. If fear left at the command of prayer, then there's a chance the fibroids could have left at the command of prayer. If the miraculous change did not happen immediately, would I have been willing to wait for manifestation? What might the outcome have been?

Is God still healing supernaturally today? Many will never know because they are impatient and run out of trust in God. In the end, I declared He is Chief Creator, Manufacturer, Distributor, and the Repairer of the breach in our souls and bodies. That is where I began my discovery because the hard times were far from over....

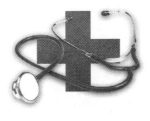

CHAPTER 3

A Moment in My Shoes

I recovered, and life was good again! I was free to resume my normal routine of work, church, and building my business. And, I did just that until business opportunities dwindled in New York. As things slowed down, I had more time to reflect on the experiences I'd endured.

Physically I was doing well. However, I wrestled mentally and emotionally with questions about life and God – what really matters?

If God is God, why do people who believe and trust in Him experience bad things in life?

I obeyed the rules of the church, but I still got sick – did I do something wrong?

Answers to those questions would come. The next stretch of my journey came first.

I continued living in New York State for a few more years but ultimately decided to relocate to Illinois in search of new work opportunities.

The move to Chicago in 1993 proved to be one of my greatest decisions. I moved in with a friend, EW. EW was the niece of my mentor, VAD. Our families were rooted in Clarksdale, MS and knew each other for many years before both EW and I were born.

As fate would have it, our family connections continued as both families continued to grow until the time when EW and I came on the scene.

EW graciously welcomed me into her home. Although short in stature, her heart was as if God created it and then said, "Supersize in generosity." She was such a giver!

EW and I were about a year apart in age and had similar interests.

We absolutely loved music. She loved to sing and played the piano, but rarely if ever shared this piece of information with anyone. I was one of the few who knew of this love of hers. The flip side of this coin is that I played piano, too. I also loved to sing, but rarely if ever, shared *this* piece of information with anyone.

EW was a person of few words. She was like E. F. Hutton – when she spoke, you listened. From what she said in any given situation, it was very clear that she had pondered the matter in her heart and for some time. Although very serious most of the time, she would oblige those around her with an occasional smile. Whenever you were successful at coaxing a smile out of her, her smile would light up the room.

The mother of two very young beautiful girls and rearing them alone, EW made room for me.

"You can stay here as long as you need to while you look for a job and a place of your own," she said.

That was unusual in the world where I lived. Outside family, I had learned not to expect such generosity and courtesy from others. I certainly would not make the mistake of taking it for granted.

"How much do I need to pay you?" I asked.

She was offended. I could tell by the frown on her face. That was the end of that discussion.

While this was a most gracious offer, my goal was to get a job and secure an apartment within 30 days. I did. How that happened was nothing short of a major blessing.

EXPECT A MIRACLE

EW worked during the day. So, her brother, JR, took me to search for an apartment. We started the search on Lake Shore Drive, a tony neighborhood stretched along Chicago's spine, near an expressway that runs alongside the Lake Michigan shoreline. He showed me this area first based on what he and EW knew about my preferred style of living and my old apartment in New York.

EW and JR were right in that Lakeshore Drive did remind me of my 17th-floor apartment in a downtown high-rise in Syracuse, New York, which had a lovely west view of the city. I'd look out of my balcony and observe Onondaga Lake at one end, the inner city, and the business district on the other. Passersby 17 floors down appeared as ants dressed in suits or casual apparel going about their daily activities.

The highlight of my day was to see the sun set. The reddish-orange and yellow, supersized beach ball hung in the sky, and at times it seemed so close that I imagined I could reach out, touch and bounce that ball high into the heavens. To finish work and other activities and make it home before sunset was indeed a treat. Often, this sight reminded me of Who created and set the sun and moon ablaze in the sky. The big, bright orange-ish and yellow sphere reminded me of Who is in control of the universe.

Lake Shore Drive is a sight to behold! However, to live there on a permanent basis will cost you a good mint. Laden with beach-front activity, skyscrapers, and luxury apartments, it's the place to be if you are a biker, jogger, walker, skater, boater, or you are loaded. A studio or efficiency apartment, about 800 square feet, back in 1993 was $900 to $1200 a month. Given the building and the view, the same accommodation in that neighborhood today goes for $1,800 to nearly $3,000. Coughing up that kind of money for less than 800 square feet did not make sense for me.

EW was at work the next time I wanted to go apartment hunting. Again, JR took me that day.

After driving through different townships, nothing readily appealed to me. Just as we were planning to head back to EW's house, finally a building caught my eye. It was a 20-unit apartment complex in Hillside. Hillside is a suburb of Chicago located about 22 miles southwest of Lake Shore Drive and 15 miles from the Loop.

I was excited because the post office was in walking distance. Small convenient stores were nearby. And, it had easy access to entertainment venues like bowling centers, theaters, miniature golf, and good restaurants all within a 5-10 mile radius. Everything I needed was right there.

This brick style apartment building had a For Rent sign and contact number written in big, bold, and white letters. It had my name written all over it! Anxiously, I jotted down the contact number and planned to inquire about availability the next day.

I did not get a lot of sleep that night. Thoughts about that apartment flooded my mind. Not having a job was on my mind, too. Truth is I didn't have a job and didn't have a lot of money saved period!

What was I thinking?

The better question is, "What was The Adversary saying to me?"

He said: "It's crazy to apply for an apartment with these realities hanging over you. No person in their right mind will give you an apartment, and you don't have a job. This is insane!"

I had applied to be a substitute teacher in several school districts but had not heard back from the Human Resources Departments. Nevertheless, encouraged within or not, I had to keep things moving.

The next day, I called the number that was on the For Rent sign. A woman by the name of Lois answered. I introduced myself to her and explained the reason for the call. She mentioned that only one apartment was vacant.

"Is it still available?" I asked.

"It's available, and it's an end unit," she replied.

"Consider this apartment taken," I said.

Those four words escaped from my mouth before I could rationalize myself out of pursuing the place. I must have been temporarily insane. In my right mind, my cautious, rational spirit would have pushed me to hang up the phone with a polite, "Oh. Well, thank you very much." Instead, I, perhaps inspired by Holy Spirit, let loose, "Consider this apartment taken."

Lois offered to meet me at the complex later in the day. I was back in my right mind again, so I told her the next day would be better for me. This way, I could drive and not be intimidated by the dark during the 14-mile trip from EW's house in Chicago to Hillside. Learning the different neighboring communities and getting from Point A to Point B was still a work in progress for me.

Given traffic activity and road conditions, the drive would take about 42 minutes on a good day.

My driving skills were exceptional – following directions, not so good. If my mind told me to go left, in all probability the correct way was to turn right. Distinguishing north, south, east, and west after the early morning or after the sun went down was impossible for me. That was my number one shortcoming in grade school. I needed sunrise and sunset to tell you the direction of those geographical points. Any other time, I could not do so without a compass.

The next day, I couldn't get dressed fast enough. As the excitement built while I prepared to meet Lois, my confidence began to deflate. In my thoughts, I asked, *How on earth are you going to pay for this apartment?* I released a long exasperated sigh. It must have lasted 30 seconds, and tears began to roll down my cheeks. Then, I prayed a simple prayer, "God, help me!"

I dried my eyes, got in the car, and set out to meet Lois. I must have looked as insecure as I felt. The woman greeted me with a hug versus a hand shake. That was unusual, but the sign of warmth helped.

She took me inside and showed me the one-bedroom apartment. The place I had claimed in faith or haste had a kitchen big enough for me to cook at the level I was going to cook - not much! The living room was spacious enough to accommodate the number of people I was accustomed to having over. Not many. The bedroom was large enough for my queen-size bed, a small sofa, and my Yamaha keyboard and recording and sound equipment.

"I want this apartment," I heard myself say. "What will it cost me, and how quickly can I move in?"

Inside, I wanted to pull every word out of the air. My heart would not allow me.

"I just moved here from New York and expect to be working as a substitute teacher in September." I went on.

That was mid-July. Worse, I was out of words. I did not want to cry.

"You look like you will pay us," Lois smiled and said as she looked into my eyes. "The apartment is yours. You'll need to give $350 deposit, and pay the first and last month's rent."

I wanted to scream and shout! This was grrrrrrrrreeeeaaaattt!

In God's Time

I moved into the apartment near the end of July 1993. Not long after, I finally got the call to start working as a substitute teacher in the Melrose Park School District. That was the area where I now lived. After a month in those schools, a local church contacted me to see if I wanted to teach in its newly established elementary school. That was a step up from subbing. I took the full-time job.

I started my new job as an elementary school teacher only to discover that the curriculum for my third-grade class was incomplete. The "must complete other assigned tasks as necessary" clause in the job description became the norm versus the exception. I found myself developing the curriculum primarily by night and continuing to create and deliver it by day in real time. My schedule started looking like the one I had when I lived in New York. The magnitude of the work was the same. The pay was far less!

Initially, I found the job to be exciting but not fulfilling. Working with learners of all ages and playing a vital role in forming their lives through education was my niche. It is who I thought I was.

Had I made the wrong decision about moving to Illinois? Was accepting this job the right thing to do? How will I make it on this level of income? I pondered these things in my heart incessantly. At one time, I thought this was what I'd do for the next 25 years and retire.

Creating lesson plans and strategic exercises for my students just wasn't hitting the spot anymore. Going to work and standing before the children every day became a chore. I felt unfulfilled and lost.

What to do next professionally weighed more heavily on my mind. There were times when I was sitting in a church service, a theater or a concert, and my mind would inevitably drift. Instead of taking in what was going on during those events, thoughts of the success I'd experienced previously seemed to play over and over again to the point of my having moved to Illinois, where I initially felt like a failure. Then, the record player in my mind would rewind and play the scenes all over again. I was on mental repeat. I knew I had to do something.

Six months later, the call for a position I had applied for earlier came through – Dean of Students for a government-funded vocational school located in downtown Chicago. That was a time when a good resume and great references could get you the job. That kind of thing is almost impossible today if you have not met a recruiter or hiring manager in person. I was practically interviewed and hired over the phone. Meeting the prospective employer was more or less a formality.

I was on my way! My primary role in this position was to advise and assist dislocated workers and help them land employment again. I was working with adults on a full-time basis. This position allowed me to combine my experience in education, business, and technology. That made me very happy, and it hit the spot.

I found a new church home, Progressive Life-Giving Word Cathedral, which I absolutely loved. In Maywood at the time, just a few miles away from where I lived, Progressive was a Word-based, spirit-filled church. The pastor, Donald L. Alford, Sr., was someone I knew of as a song writer and musician when I lived in Mississippi in the 1980s. I purchased his music albums. Vinyl and 8 tracks were the primary media during this time. I had no clue that he would become a pastor and that I at some point in time would become a member of his church.

Pastor Alford was a man of integrity, a true worshiper, who came highly recommended by my mentor, VAD. She knew and trusted the leaders there and thought it would be a healthy environment for me. She often ministered there prior to my becoming a member and continued to do so afterward. After visiting, I was convinced that joining this ministry was the right thing to do. I felt right at home.

The organizational structure of this church was familiar to me. It was formerly a part of the Church of God in Christ organization but had transitioned to a non-denominational organization by the time I made my visit. The last church I'd attended in my hometown of Clarksdale, Mississippi, and the one in Syracuse, New York were also a part of the Church of God in Christ organization. Although Progressive had become non-denominational, I was comfortable there.

The older, seasoned women, commonly referred to as Church Mothers, nurtured and loved unconditionally. With Dad no longer living and Mom living in Mississippi, having relationships with the individuals at this ministry helped to fill the void of my not having seasoned influence and guidance from folks my parents' age – people that had been where I was trying to go naturally and spiritually. On those occasions when I did not travel home for major holidays due to inclement weather, it was OK because I always had an invitation to spend this time with at least one family from the church. Life was good!

About four years later I'd moved on to a better job with increased pay and bought a new home. There were no major sinus flare-ups like the ones that plagued me in New York State. I cannot explain how the move to Illinois made such a difference. It remains a mystery! All I can say is that it was a beautiful stretch of time without having a stuffy or runny nose, pain over the nose bridge especially when blowing, constant sneezing or coughing (sometimes with a bloody discharge).

By my twelfth year of living in Illinois and two homes later, I'd gotten accustomed to living life without any major health issues. As the thirteenth year set in, and for no apparent reason, things began to change. Problems with my sinuses arose and with a vengeance. It seemed as if every three months or when the seasons changed, they became extremely inflamed and irritated. I sneezed uncontrollably throughout the day. My eyes teared constantly. They were red, itchy, swollen, and blurry most of the time. I had headaches that grew intense. I became extremely sensitive to sound. My head would split at the sound of a feather hitting the floor. I was tired all the time with little to no energy to make it through an entire day. To make matters worse, I had a gut-wrenching, uncontrollable, non-producing, dry cough. This cough was more severe than what I'd experienced when I lived in New York State. It sounded like I was coughing my insides out. It was so embarrassing!

Most of my work involved face-to-face interaction. During this time, I was responsible for delivering onsite customer training. When I was not training, I was in a lot of meetings regarding the accounts of different clients. Whether I had to speak or not, I was uncomfortable because of the cough. In fact, I think it made others uncomfortable, too.

In the back of my mind I wondered what they were saying about my cough and me. Did they think I had an incurable disease? Did they think I had something that was contagious?

This was nothing new. I fought with sinus issues ever since I moved from Mississippi to New York in 1986 to find a job in my field. But, now in 2006, something more vicious than the sinus issues attacked my body. It seemed like the typical cold or sinusitis but proved to be something greater. Nonetheless, I had had enough!

I had become more knowledgeable about how The Adversary works. In my case, The Adversary used sickness in an attempt to get me to change my confession about God, much like how he did with Job in the Bible.

Job was blameless and upright; he feared God and shunned evil. He had many blessings: seven sons and three daughters, seven thousand sheep, three thousand camels, five hundred yoke of oxen, five hundred donkeys, and a large number of servants. During his day, Job may have been the richest man on the face of the earth. Because of this, he got The Adversary's attention.

Satan says to God in Job 1:9-11:

> "Does Job fear God for nought (nothing)? Hast thou not made a hedge about him, and about his house, and about all that he hath on every side? Thou hast blessed the work of his hands, and his substance is increased in the land. But put forth thine hand now, and touch all that he hath, and he will curse thee to thy face."

God challenged the "accuser of the brethren." As the story continues, God says to Satan, "Everything Job has is in your power, but on the man himself do not lay a finger on him" (Job 1:12). Now with total access to all of Job's possessions, The Adversary took Job's oxen, sheep, camels, servants, and even his children. But, instead of making a U-turn in his faith, Job worshipped God even more.

"Naked I came from my mother's womb, and naked shall I return," he said. "The Lord giveth, and the Lord taketh away; Blessed be the name of the Lord. In all of this, Job did not sin nor charge God foolishly" (Job 1:20-22). Job kept the faith. Now it was my turn.

Although not as severe as how he had attacked Job, The Adversary tested my faith. Never did he use the phrase, "Curse God and follow me." He tried to plant thoughts in my mind that suggested God does not keep His promises or do what He says He will do. The Adversary suggested thoughts to me in the form of a question just as he used to deceive Eve in Genesis 3:1-7.

> "Now the serpent was more subtil than any beast of the field which the LORD God had made. And he said unto the woman, Yea, hath God said, Ye shall not eat of every tree of the garden? And the woman said unto the serpent, we may eat of the fruit of the trees of the

garden: But of the fruit of the tree which is in the midst of the garden, God hath said, Ye shall not eat of it, neither shall ye touch it, lest ye die. And the serpent said unto the woman, Ye shall not surely die: For God doth know that in the day ye eat thereof, then your eyes shall be opened, and ye shall be as gods, knowing good and evil. And when the woman saw that the tree was good for food, and that it was pleasant to the eyes, and a tree to be desired to make one wise, she took of the fruit thereof, and did eat, and gave also unto her husband with her; and he did eat. And the eyes of them both were opened, and they knew that they were naked; and they sewed fig leaves together, and made themselves aprons."

The Adversary came at me with questions like, "Do you really believe God loves you? Do you think he would heal you and you missed church the other week? Why would you believe Him? By the way, if He cared so much about you, why are you having all these challenges?"

These questions were designed to create doubt. The Adversary's goal was to thwart the potential of what my faith could produce over time as I continued my walk and growth in Christ. It is through this situation that I learned that while standing in faith will sometimes hurt, it is still the best posture.

The dry, uncontrollable cough that advanced to the ugly cough was accompanied by a running nose, tearing eyes, aching muscles, and graduated to what resembled a full-blown sinus infection. I tried over-the-counter drugs to bring this under control but nothing worked. So, I called my doctor's office and was able to schedule an appointment for the next day.

Dr. P. did her routine checkup and concluded it was a sinus infection wreaking havoc in my body. By this time, walking and sitting up were hard to do. She gave me antibiotics, a nasal spray, and an inhaler and explained how and when to take each. I left and continued the regimen according to her instructions.

While this combination of pharmaceuticals usually worked for me, this time it did not. Three days had passed and I wasn't getting better. On the fourth day, I did a walk-in to Dr. P.'s office only to discover she was out for the day. The receptionist found an opening for me to see Dr. P.'s nurse. We discussed what was going on – I told her the meds I'd received a few days ago were not working. In fact, "I am feeling worse" is what I told the nurse. She contacted Dr. P. and explained the situation. Dr. P. prescribed a different antibiotic and inhaler.

Feeling hopeful, I left and picked up my prescriptions on the way home. My hope failed by 9 p.m. that night. By that time, a new symptom emerged. Every time I coughed, pain raced through my body and abruptly paralyzed my ability to breathe. I could not even make a subtle movement without experiencing pain. This felt like what many people describe as a heart attack. This had never happened before.

Am I having a heart attack...what is this? I thought.

Immediately, I started looking for ways to ease the pain. I sat up in the bed. That didn't work. I laid on my back. That was a mistake. The pressure resulting from the cough in that position was terrible. Finally, I tried lying on my stomach. That helped! But, I still thought, *Am I having a heart attack or stroke?*

I concluded that this could not be because the pain subsided when I lay on my stomach and coughed. From what I knew about a heart attack, chest pain is continuous.

Have you ever been so sick you could not see straight? Think straight? Sit up? Lie down? Call somebody? Pray for yourself?

I should have called 911 or gone to the ER. I wasn't feeling well enough to do either.

I now advise you to *immediately* seek help if you find yourself in such a situation. I would have if I had known what was about to happen.

Not really knowing what to do next and hoping the new medication would kick in soon, I decided to go to bed. As I prepared for bed that night, as sure as my name is Jacquelyn (a.k.a., Jackie), I heard a voice in my inner ear tell me:

1. Pack a bag.
2. Set up automatic bill pay on all of your accounts.
3. Be at the doctor's office by 8 a.m.
4. Make a list of the names of your sisters and other key information your friends and family will need to know.

What is going on here? I thought.

Looking back, it was Holy Spirit preparing me for what was ahead. In retrospect I asked, "If Holy Spirit could tell me to do all of this, why couldn't He just instantly heal my body?"

Today, I better understand Holy Spirit was giving me a part of the protocol for a healing journey. Those instructions set the stage for preparation for change that would be manifested in my body over time.

It is through this experience that I learned that not all healing is manifested instantly. As believers, we must be careful not to dismiss the abilities God has given to physicians and other medical professionals to help us manage medical issues on a day-to-day basis. After all, Luke, one of Jesus' twelve disciples, was a physician, too. Scripture does not say he abandoned those skills simply because he was called to follow Jesus and become an apostle. We must be open to how God chooses to allow healing to manifest in our bodies, or we might miss it altogether. Some miss it because they do not immediately see signs of supernatural healing after they've prayed, and they refuse the protocol of physicians – God sometimes uses the knowledge and protocol of physicians to reveal what ails us and to administer health and healing for our bodies.

We don't need to focus on how He will do it. We just need to put our trust in the belief that He wants us healthy – He wants us healed – He wants us well. We need to put our trust in the belief that He is able to make us healthy. We need to trust and believe that He will do that for us. He will manifest what He has already done.

Our Father's promises are written in eternal ink – His promises are already kept. They are waiting for us to activate them in time through faith.

THE ROUGH SIDE OF THE MOUNTAIN

With packed bags in the car and my list of "Who to call in case of emergency…" in hand, I arrived at the doctor's office at 8 a.m. I felt worse than ever. By this time, I was wheezing, extremely weak, and could barely walk or talk. With each cough, it felt as if I was going to pass out.

With my head hanging down, I made my way to the front desk. "May I help you," said one of the receptionists. As I looked up and attempted to answer her, the look on her face and others working in that area went from a happy-like look to a very concerned look. I whispered to the receptionist, "I need help."

I barely got those words out. Tears began to stream down my face. The receptionist immediately came to assist me where I stood at the window of the intake room. Even as I write this section, tears come to my eyes, along with a "thank-you," and a lump in my throat, as I remember how the staff saw my need and urgently took the necessary steps to respond. Normally, I would have had to fill out paperwork before I could see the doctor. This time, the nurse didn't even mention paperwork and immediately took me into a room to wait for Dr. P. She took my blood pressure and temperature but never told me what the numbers were; nor did I ask as I normally did. I was too sick to care at this point!

She logged her findings and told me to relax. She told me the doctor was finishing a visit with another patient and that she would see me next.

About five to ten minutes had passed before Dr. P. arrived. She greeted me warmly but with concern. I imagine the concern was a combination of my being there a third time and whatever she saw in my blood pressure and temperature readings. Dr. P. eased into asking me questions about what had gone on with my last two visits as she, herself, took my vitals. Normally, she would tell me what the readings were, but this time she did not share her findings. I'm thinking, *"That's unusual."* Everything in me wanted to know those findings. Truth be told, I was in too much discomfort to inquire about her findings as I usually did along with asking about fifty other questions. I was hungry, very hot, and extremely irritable. If they didn't mention the readings, I wouldn't ask what they were. I let it pass.

The pain from the cough was getting worse. I had become somewhat shaky. The best thing for me to do was switch from sitting up to lying on my stomach. I remained in that position for the duration of the appointment. Dr. P. instructed me to rest for a few minutes longer. She said she needed to check on something and would return shortly but did not explain in any detail as to what that something was.

I thought – *Maybe she stepped out to try to stay on schedule in seeing her other patients or she needed to seek the opinion of another physician.*

About fifteen minutes passed before Dr. P. returned. She took my blood pressure and temperature again. Then, she indicated she needed to step out yet again and would return shortly. She left the room. She returned in about fifteen minutes. She took my temperature and blood pressure again. This went on several more times. But, when it occurred at what would become the last time, I realized that I had been there about an hour and a half. I thought to myself and even muttered under my breath, *"This is a very long time for a regular doctor's office visit – I'm ready to go home."* Typically, a session with my doctor would last 15 – 20 minutes. So, this time I asked, "Dr. P., what's going on?"

"Do you have someone you can call to be with you?" she asked.

"Do I have someone I can call to be with me?" I repeated. "Why do I need someone to be with me?"

Dr. P. began to explain, "Your temperature is fluctuating. Right now it is over 101 degrees, your heart is beating too fast, and your blood pressure is very high."

"What about my blood pressure?" I interrupted.

"Your blood pressure is too high," she continued. "The normal range for a person your age is between 110/70 and 120/80. Yours is very high."

I was 40. My blood pressure was above the high end of the range. It kept getting higher.

The blood pressure thing got to me. I got upset because "Flashback" paid me a visit.

> *You know your dad had hypertension and died of a heart attack,* Flashback said. *Your mom died from congestive heart disease. Your brother, Al, had what your mom had. He died of a heart attack, too.*

Flashback tried to keep talking, but I silenced him, even in my weakness. If I was going to make it through this ordeal, I had learned from my previous medical battles that I had to quickly shut down the negative thoughts. I had to feed my faith and not submit to any negative thinking.

"I cannot let you go home," said Dr. P. "I've got to send you to the hospital for further observation because I can't determine what is going on with the limited tools we have here in the office. So, call your friends and have them come and take you to the ER as I prepare them for your arrival."

I must have been in a really bad condition because I did not resist those instructions. My friend, GR, was preparing to go out of town the day all this happened. So, I had to call on my friend, Dorothy (DJ). I called DJ to let her know something was going on even though I did not have all of the facts. DJ was in my immediate circle of friends that spent a lot of quality time together almost every week. There wasn't a week in the month that went by without our getting together for good food, good fun, and great fellowship. We ate together, had Bible study in one another's homes, we prayed, cried, and laughed together. We represented four decades – one was in her 30s. I was in my 40s. Another was in her 50s, and DJ, in her 60s, was the senior in the group. She was a very caring person who would indeed give her very last if she knew you were in need. When she gave of her time, money, or resources, she expected nothing in return but for you to pay it forward.

DJ answered the phone with a chipper voice. Hello, Dr. Golden," she said. "Hey DJ! I am at the doctor's office, and my doctor says I need to go to the ER."

She asked, "What's going on?"

"I came in because I was having problems with my sinuses and started having chest pains. When they checked my blood pressure and temperature, both were too high – so high that my doctor said that legally she cannot release me to go home," I explained. Very calmly, DJ said, "Give me the address; I am on my way." She ended the call by saying, "I'll call the others (those in our circle of friends), so they can begin to pray."

SIDEBAR

Always have one or two people in your life who will show up on your behalf – someone from your family, church, or workplace. And, if they cannot show up, make sure they have someone they can entrust your life to in their absence. You will need them.

As I waited for DJ, I was calm and resting. Thinking ahead, I thought I'd be at the Emergency Room for a short while, and then the doctors would release me to go home. I was so sure that I planned for DJ and me to stop and have dinner together. Oh! How wrong I was.

DJ showed up about twenty minutes after our call, and the receptionist escorted her to the examination room where I was resting. Boy, was I glad to see her! I was afraid, but this time I was not paralyzed in my thinking as I'd experienced in times past. I was immediately comforted as she grabbed me by the hand and asked if I knew more than what I'd shared on the phone. I told her, "No, the doctor still wants me to go to the hospital." Just as I was telling her this, Dr. P. entered the room and introduced herself. She restated what I'd already shared with DJ and instructed her to get me to the hospital as quickly as possible. She stated emphatically, "By all means, do not let Jackie talk you into taking her home."

Remember the bag I packed earlier? Well, DJ got that bag from my car and proceeded to take me to the hospital. To my surprise, they admitted me. I was an independent technical training consultant. I had insurance, but the benefits were vastly different from what a full-time, employee, group insurance program offered.

Now, The Adversary is costing me money! *I said to myself.* I'm not liking this.

BLESSINGS OVERFLOW

After waiting in the emergency room for what seemed to be forever, the hospital staff finally completed the admissions process and transported me to a room. With this behind me, suddenly I remembered I was supposed to be at work! Talk about panic! I had only been on my new work assignment as a consultant for ten months.

They're going to end my contract and replace me, I thought.

I snapped into being more alert long enough to give the office a call – I had to talk to my manager, Karen.

"Hi Karen, this is Jackie," I said in my now almost baritone voice. I had coughed so much that my usual contralto voice fell a few levels.

"Jackie, what's the matter?" Karen sounded alarmed and called my name in a concerned tone.

I explained to her that I had been admitted to the hospital. "As soon as I know more, I'll give you a call," I told her.

My intention was not to call Karen until I knew exactly what was going on in my body and when I knew when I was on my way home. It didn't quite turn out that way. Thoughts about work kept coming to my mind. Each time they did, I was compelled to call. By the third call, Karen told me to take the time I need to deal with this situation and not to worry about calling in to give updates.

"We just want you well," she said emphatically.

By now my cell phone, the telephone in my room and at the nurses' station were ringing off the hook. I had only been in the hospital room about three hours or so. All of my siblings (10 of 13 at the time), cousins, colleagues, and church families past and present were calling to check on me. I was happy to know that people cared, but at the same time I struggled with trying to be strong. DJ was with me, so for the most part I was OK. She answered each call and announced each caller. If the physicians or nurses were not attending to me, I'd take the call.

My niece Nigel (pronounced "knee gail") called, and I was free to talk to her. I could hear her fighting to hold back the tears; however, some of them got away. She was very concerned and afraid for me. And, when I heard her say, "Aunt Jackie, are you gonna be OK?" I, too, almost shed some tears. Instead, I transitioned into "auntie and protector" mode. The fight in me to comfort her began to rise. "Yes! I will be alright – this is temporary," I exclaimed. "I'm gonna be OK."

Nigel might have thought she was being weak. If that were true, it was her weakness that reminded me that I wanted to live and beat whatever was causing these issues in my body. It was her transparency that reminded me of the power that I needed to tap into if I was going to be alright.

Behind the scenes, I had a number of friends working on my behalf. It was like an assembly line of individuals working toward a common goal to make sure everything that concerned me was handled in a way that I could be at peace. I cannot recall all who came to my aid, but I will never forget their deeds.

Here's what I remembered. I gave the keys to my home and car along with a list of whom to call to my friend, BW, who was the youngest in my friendship circle I mentioned earlier. She was a smart, young business woman known to make things happen. If there was anyone who could bring order to a chaotic situation, BW was the one for the job. She had thick skin, which automatically qualified her for the strong personalities she was about to encounter.

There was another friend, GA, who was very involved in this process. I call her my "storm carrier." When I had to bury Mom in 1996, it was GA who was by my side to comfort me. If you think that is something, she had recruited another dear friend, DM, to accompany her and lend her support and comfort as well. Finding myself in need of this same level of love and support again, GA stepped into that role once more. Knowing that two of my sisters were on their way to be with me, she made the arrangements to transport them from the airport to the hospital.

While these things were going on, DJ left the hospital but called my pastor to make him aware of the situation. He notified the church family. Together, they made sure someone was with me until my relatives arrived from out of town and could take control of the situation.

Their participation in my journey did not end there.

The driver who GA arranged to pick up my sister Earline – the eldest of my six sisters – dropped her off at the hospital. BW met her there. After she got an assessment of what was going on, which was no more than what I had already shared with her, BW took her to my house to let her orient herself and made sure she knew how to get to and from the hospital.

The hospital stay kicked into full motion. Between staff, family, and visitors, the traffic in and out of my room drastically increased. Doctors and nurses were coming in and out every five to fifteen minutes. The nurses took turns trying to find a vein that would allow them to take blood samples. Several times they failed because I was somewhat dehydrated. Eventually, they were able to draw blood and hook up the IV to get the fluid intake going.

As nightfall approached, my situation did not improve. I could no longer control my bodily functions. My temperature continued to rise. My blood pressure would not stabilize. The medicine used to control the blood pressure caused my sugar levels to increase. So, now I was on the verge of becoming diabetic. The coughing got worse. The chest pains grew more severe.

Throughout my hospital stay until I went home and was able to return to work, members from my old and new church visited me to make sure I was doing well. On occasion when I awakened, my pastor NM and his wife GM were sitting by my side. I was happy to see them but also thought *if they are here, I must be in really bad shape.* Then, I would drift back into an unconscious-like state.

Time continued to move on, and by this time I was coughing up a rib (at least that is what it felt like). I was starving because they wouldn't give me food. Because I had lost control of my bodily functions, the lead attending physician would not permit me to eat solid food until they determined what was going on. There I lay hungry, frustrated, sleepy, irritable, unable to control my body, and having to rely on a portable toilet when I needed to relieve myself. This was most embarrassing. With visitors and the medical staff coming in and out, using a bedside toilet was not something I desired – I didn't care how sick I was. That just wasn't cool!

Two days went by, and I still had not gone to sleep. The pain continued to intensify even after being on morphine since I'd been admitted. It advanced to the point that my doctor tripled the dosage of morphine so that I could get some relief. Each time my primary nurse came to check my blood pressure, sugar level, and temperature, she suggested I try to sleep. I could not. Finally, she told the doctor that I needed something to help me sleep. At her recommendation, my doctor added a sleeping pill to the mix to help me get the rest I so desperately needed.

At last, I went to sleep after about an hour after taking the sleeping pill. But, what an experience that was! It was a night of horror for me.

While sleeping, it seemed as if every machine I was hooked up to was talking to me. I was dreaming. And, what I dreamed actually happened – IN PART.

A WALK IN A CLOUD

There I stood in a daze as my eyes traced the path of blood that had spilled all over the bed. The once pure-white sheets were saturated with rich, red blood. The floor was covered in blood, and bloody foot prints led from my room, down the hall, and to the nurses' station. I was being held in the hospital under protective custody but somehow got away. As I walked in the bloody steps, it occurred to me that the size of the footprint matched mine. In reality the nurses' station was just outside my room in the Intensive Care Unit, but in the dream it seemed as if I had to walk about five minutes down a long hallway to get there.

I recall standing at the nurses' station. Terrified and crying profusely, I could hear myself telling the nurses, "I would never do anything like this. I love God too much to do this. I did not do it! I did not kill that person!" The dream continued, but this is all I remember.

The next day after I had awakened, my primary nurse entered the room. Immediately, I began to tell her about what had happened (keep in mind I was still under the impression that I had killed someone, so I very skillfully brought up the subject by asking questions). I asked if she had seen all that blood, and I was sorry she had to clean up the mess that someone had made. Somewhat reluctantly, she eased into a reply telling me that she had indeed been the one to clean up the room.

"What!" I said. "You are kidding, right? What happened?"

"No, I'm not kidding," she replied. "You were dreaming, but the blood was real. The blood was your blood. While you were asleep last night, you pulled out the IV and anything connected to your body. You got out the bed. Then, you started walking out the door and headed across the hallway to the nurses' station. Fortunately, I was on my way to check on you. We took you back to your room, changed the sheets, and got your IV and everything else set up again. We were hoping you would not remember this because we thought it would be too traumatic for you. But, I think you need to know that you DID NOT kill anyone – it was all a dream and side effects of the medication."

Side effects of the medication, I exclaimed loudly in my mind.

The nurse assured me again that I had not killed anyone. The Secret Service was not standing guard at the door of my hospital room. Those memories were just a part of the dream. Unfortunately, those memories would impact my trust in the medications that the doctors would prescribe moving forward.

After I became restless again, my nurse asked if I wanted the doctor to prescribe a different sleeping aid for me. Needless to say, I refused it and any other kind of pill. I was not taking any more medication until I understood all of the potential side effects.

BW came to visit. I told her about my eventful night. As fate would have it, the doctors came to do their rounds when she and my sister were there. BW took it upon herself to tell the doctors not to give me any strong medication unless it was needed to save my life.

"I can barely get Jackie to take an aspirin for a headache," she told them. "She is not accustomed to taking strong medication of any kind."

She looked at my sister, Earline, a former nurse. "I live with Jackie every day," she told her. Don't let them do this!" My sister took note. The nurse in her took us the rest of the way in this journey.

As my hospital stay continued, I became more and more frustrated. Each time I asked what was wrong with me, no one could tell me anything definitive. All I knew was that the doctors could not regulate my blood pressure and temperature. According to the doctors, my immune system had gone into attack mode and was waging war on my body in an effort to heal itself.

That phrase (heal itself) should have jogged my spiritual memory. It did not, because by that time, I was in and out of an unconscious-like state so much, nothing was really clear. Sometimes I could speak intelligibly and question my doctors and nurses about my condition and the medications. Often, these exchanges would end on a not-so-happy note because all that the doctors wanted to do was get my situation under control. All *I* wanted to do was get me fixed fast, take as few pills as possible, and go home.

At other times, I tried to maintain my physical appearance. This was difficult because I was on bed rest and hooked up to a lot of machines. So, I was not free to move around as I desired. Being the appearance-conscientious person I was, the last thing I wanted to do was look like I actually felt! So, out came the make-up bag, comb, and brush whenever I had a good moment. Looking good, in the sense of not looking sickly, was as important to me as actually getting well.

It was a wild experience. The uncertainties of the situation were so weird that one of the attending physicians accused me of faking the illness. He entered my room one day AND saw me applying either lip stick or lip balm. I was momentarily "with it" enough to ask him intelligent questions about what was going on with my body, so he concluded my illness was a fake. I did not challenge him because I was just too sick. My "big sister," Earline was on the scene. I was confident she would handle this and all things moving forward.

Now, let me tell you what my sister told me about the person I'd become during this hospital stay. It was kind of funny, but not really. I had become the Incredible Hulk. She said I'd transformed into a green, mean monster. In her words, I was so picky that it came across as if I were inherently a mean person. Music was playing, and I did not want to hear music. Those who knew me knew I absolutely love music. At times the television was on my favorite stations where you could watch *Leave It to Beaver, Family Affair, The Andy Griffith Show, My Three Sons, Petticoat Junction, The Cosby Show, and A Different World*, the oldies if you will. I did not want the television to be on those stations, nor any station for that matter. All of this should have let somebody know something was really wrong with me.

A lot of people visited me. For this I am very appreciative to this day. Unfortunately, I was in and out of it much of the time and can't remember all who came. I do remember the level of collective concern - and perhaps over-concern - as some aggressively prayed over me. I was not in the mood for that. That's right!

There were not a lot of people who responded in this fashion, but when you are sick, all it takes is one person to approach you the wrong way or do the wrong thing, and it can add misery to the already-exasperating situation. This saved, anointed believer, and minister of the Gospel was not in the mood for anyone standing over her and praying at the top of their voice. To be totally honest, I could not direct my mind toward prayer at this time, and soft prayer hurt if you know what I mean.

Praying loudly doesn't necessarily move the hand of God on one's behalf. And, while the matter may be one of urgency, decency and order should still rule. What makes the difference in a situation like this is the combination of prayers that were set in motion before the adverse situation started, continued momentum of prayer, and the collective fervency of those prayers that deal head-on with trouble when you do not have the wherewithal to pray for yourself. How loudly one prays is not the key.

Sidebar

Consider this. When people are gravely ill, they may respond differently from how you may be accustomed to seeing them act on a day-to-day basis. In my case, I was not the happy person that I generally was. My level of tolerance had diminished. Sometimes I could not stand for anyone to talk to me or touch me. Short conversations about the simplest things annoyed me. For example, "Do you want me to turn on some music?" asked my sister Sue in attempt to simply help me. I became angry as she put the TV on the music channel and in a very ugly tone said, "Turn it off!" In retrospect, I know she was just trying to do what she thought I would have wanted.

Sometimes my visitors' cologne, perfume, or body lotion fragrance made me nauseous. I remember thinking, one day I am going to write a book about hospital bedside protocol and etiquette. *In my observation in general, we need to be more sensitive and conscientious in how to care for the critically ill.*

Sometimes the best way to care for the sick is to just show up and not say more than "Hello – do you need anything?"

If the patient says no, then say, "OK, I'll be sitting in the corner if you do."

Some people act the way they do toward patients to satisfy themselves when they should keep that person's needs in focus. Remember, it is not about you.

Sometimes all that is required in caring for the sick is to give them a few minutes alone throughout the time you are visiting. Unless you are designated to spend the night, consider staggering the amount of time you spend during your visit. Limit the time you are with the patient from 15 to 30 minutes at the most. Or, if you plan to visit with them longer, manage your presence with intentional silence during your stay.

Sometimes it is simply turning the lights down or turning them off altogether that makes the difference for the one lying in that bed. You may think it is good to let a little sunshine in, and yes, on a normal day for that person it is. In some instances, the sick person is thinking that light is really hurting his or her eyes. The bottom line is that the needs of each individual person will vary. How a sick person responds may be atypical and not the behavior you would normally expect from them in their current situation.

Earline continued to tell me about this person I had become. Nothing made me happy. Nothing satisfied me. I was ordering people around as if I were Sargeant Jackie, and new recruits had just arrived for boot camp.

This, I sort of remember but not totally, and certainly I am not proud of this behavior. Yet, I was dealing with issues that were not always obvious to the casual observer.

One minute I was cold, and within the same minute I became hot. The hospital beds were not comfortable to me. I started out with the type that automatically shifts you so you would not develop bed sores. I remember being moved from that bed to a different one, but to me it was not firm enough. That one was not comfortable, so they switched me to a bed with a firmer mattress. Finally, we thought we found one just right for me, and it was, but the pillows were not right. Keep in mind, they were the same pillows with which I previously had no issues.

So, the hospital staff must have switched my bed at least three times. I think I ended up with about six pillows. Had I known they were charging me for each switch and fluffing of my pillows, I probably would have adapted to the first bed they gave me – but that's my sober mind's thinking today. The bed situation was so frustrating that to this day, I cannot sleep in my own bed if it's turned in a certain direction in my bedroom.

The list of frustrations went on and on. Oh! Did I tell you they still wouldn't give me any real food? Right! They only gave me broth! Steak-flavored broth! Chicken-flavored broth! Can I tell you this – "Flavor is not food, and it sure doesn't fill you up!"

CHAPTER 4

Being Human

The Adversary, the devil, tried to make me believe I was sicker than I had ever been in my life. This enemy tried to make me change my confession. The Adversary tried to get me to say with my own mouth something other than what God had said to me about me.

"You have not been on your job that long," I heard him say. "Now you are missing all this time. You are going to lose your job. You won't be able to pay your bills. No job? You can't pay your mortgage and car note. The doctors can't figure out what is wrong with you. You are going to die. You might as well give up."

I was not surprised. The Bible tells many stories of temptation. The Enemy even tried his wiles on the Son of God. Matthew 4: 1-11 (English Standard Version) states:

> Then Jesus was led up by the Spirit into the wilderness to be tempted by the devil. And after fasting forty days and forty nights, he was hungry.
>
> And the tempter came and said to him, "If you are the Son of God, command these stones to become loaves of bread."
>
> But he answered, "It is written, 'Man shall not live by bread alone, but by every word that comes from the mouth of God.'"
>
> Then the devil took him to the holy city and set him on the pinnacle of the temple and said to him, "If you are the Son of God, throw yourself down," for it is written,

>"'He will command his angels concerning you, and on their hands they will bear you up, lest you strike your foot against a stone.'"
>
>Jesus said to him, "Again it is written, 'You shall not put the Lord your God to the test.'"
>
>Again, the devil took him to a very high mountain and showed him all the kingdoms of the world and their glory. And he said to him, "All these I will give you, if you will fall down and worship me."
>
>Then Jesus said to him, "Be gone, Satan! For it is written, 'You shall worship the Lord your God and him only shall you serve.'"
>
>Then the devil left him, and behold, angels came and were ministering to him.

If He who was the Word had to use the Word to resist temptation and the lies the devil brought to Him, how much more are we to do the same?

So, giving up was also not an option for me. That joker should have knocked me out when I did not know how to execute my faith. At this stage of the game, I had learned too much. I had experienced the healing power of God. Death did not scare me. If I died, I would be in the presence of the Lord. "In the end, I win," was my resolve.

Research shows that as human beings, we are more inclined to believe what we hear ourselves say than we are to believe what we hear others say. The Adversary knows this and takes full advantage of that fact on a daily basis. I call his strategy KSD – Kill, Steal, and Destroy. In many cases, he succeeds by getting into the voice of our minds. He repeatedly feeds us these negative thoughts until the voice begins to feel as if one is speaking to oneself. I was a human under attack by The Adversary.

A Friend in Deed

Another part of the problem, inadvertently of course, came from the people trying to help me.

Some did help the way I needed; others in ways *they* wanted. I learned that if you are going to help someone who is very ill, and it is within your means, you must help them the way they want as long as that does not contribute to the illness, and the assistance does not mentally, physically, emotionally, or spiritually violate you. The situation is not about you. What you think individuals prefer when they are well might vary when they deal with conditions that try to take them out of this world. Sickness takes a toll on the mind, body, and emotions. So, anyone who lends a hand must take this into consideration if the goal is to meet the person's need.

At this point, I have no clue as to what day of the total twelve days I am on in sharing this experience with you. I believe it was Day 2 or 3. The doctor tried to give me a colonoscopy. All I wanted to do was sleep. Being sleepy and having to prep for this procedure at the same time did not mix very well.

A Pot to...

Earline stayed awake all night. Every 15 minutes or so, she would wake me up so that I could drink the "nasty stuff," a laxative, you have to drink before you undergo a procedure like a colonoscopy. I already couldn't control my bodily functions. What made matters worse – I was not free to use a normal bathroom.

I had to resort to a bedside toilet or bed pan. It wasn't a pretty picture. As I now describe the experience when kidding around with my friends, I sum it up like this: "It was awFULL...that's A-W-F-U-L-L! – just awFULL." As sick as I was, there was still a part of my dignity that I could not relinquish and fought hard to retain. That's just how I am wired. I like things done in a certain way. Using a portable toilet in an open room where at any moment someone could walk in simply did not appeal to me. Ultimately, I had to give up this expectation because getting me well was the priority, not maintaining my pride.

We got as much of the nasty stuff in me as was possible. Because I was bleeding internally, the doctor could only do a partial colonoscopy. He could not readily determine the source of the bleeding and decided not to proceed any further. The way he described it, things looked really bad, and where the blood was coming from was undetectable. There were polyps. My immune system fought harder and harder against the body's attempt to heal itself.

What was pushing my immune system into overdrive? I'd never heard of such a thing!

Other respiratory test results arrived. They revealed that pneumonia played a part. My lungs were filled with fluid. My temperature was very high. My blood pressure was out of control, and my pulse was racing. At several points, they thought they were losing me. The truth of the matter is they were.

I was being human. My present state was fragile. The future was not promised.

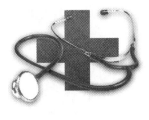

CHAPTER 5

Storm Carriers

There is no doubt. I felt like the Apostles in a boat on a stormy sea. Matthew 8:23-27 (ESV) records that Jesus' followers witnessed the Master perform healings and other miracles, yet like me in my hospital bed, they were scared out of their minds. Verse 27 says the disciples exclaimed, "What sort of man is this, that even winds and sea obey him?"

I was about to find out. Also, He showed me the beauty and benefit of angels.

Earline, who came all the way from suburban Detroit to be at my beck and call, was 64 with her own illnesses, but she stayed by my side night and day. Without complaint, she slept on a hospital cot or in a chair ten of the twelve days I was in the hospital. Ninety-nine percent of that time, this volunteer guardian only ate hospital food. Now to be fair and frank, this hospital's cuisine was an exception to the familiar, flavorless norm. The food was actually good and was as close to a home-cooked meal as one could get without having the real thing. I learned this when I visited others there and had some food, not because they fed me during my twelve days! It wasn't until near the end of my stay that they fed me real, solid food. At that point, anything solid tasted like fine cuisine. Nonetheless, you know there is nothing that compares to a real, good, home-cooked meal.

THE GODSEND

Like Jesus in Matthew 23, my sister Earline, a companion in "the boat," shared my journey through the storm. Like the disciples, I pleaded with Jesus to save me from the furious tides of weakness, pain, and fear that swirled about us. In this Bible story, Jesus awakened and calmed the troubled waters. He rescued the disciples. He sent me DJ.

Without fanfare, my friend, DJ, did something to change our view and spur hope. Never once focusing on her own life's issues in the midst of my storm, she who had become a storm carrier in my life came in with a bounce of happy in her step, carrying picnic baskets, containers, and a smile. I'll never forget, in one container, there was roast beef with gravy and baked chicken. Macaroni and cheese, fresh corn, sweet potatoes, and either cornbread or rolls were in another. There were fresh string beans and greens. To top it all off, I remember peach cobbler.

Oh! How the aroma filled my room. My taste buds stood at attention. Sad to say, all I could have was the aroma. I couldn't keep solids down so I quickly perished that thought. After all, it was my sister for whom DJ had prepared the spread! In my mind I thought: *She knows I can't eat this food*. Truth is she did know.

She explained, "I wanted to make sure Earline was OK. I want to make sure she had a break from eating hospital food."

Being an exceptional cook herself, Earline knew good cooking before ever tasting it. From the look on her face and the tears that flowed from her eyes as she took her first bite, I knew something special was taking place. I did not interrupt the moment. I just smiled within and let the moment unfold.

There was another container nicely tucked away. I thought maybe it was my favorite, German chocolate cake. Hint, hint! The surprise was not a cake. It was something greater.

The box had plates made of china and real silverware. There were cloth napkins adorned with vibrant colors that lingered in the mind's eye. You could not forget them, even when you looked away. Red, yellow, and blue never looked that bright to me before. They shone as if those napkins had a glowing effect on them.

What appeared to be a person bringing a meal to another was in truth far more than met the eye. I don't know if DJ knew, but she did more than attend to my sister's physical need. She helped her spiritually, mentally, and emotionally. She took the time to minister to the one who was ministering. DJ's unselfishness and generosity massaged my sister's heart. Even though my sister was an experienced and extremely skilled nurse for more than 20 years and had weathered storms personally and professionally, things are different when your youngest sibling lies in a bed, and you do not know whether she will live or die.

DJ stepped in and marked our lives for life. Contrary to popular belief in our society that highly prizes individualism, we all need somebody on whom to lean and depend. Like the others who came to my rescue, DJ was the epitome of a storm carrier. She who acted on faith to meet a friend's unspoken needs while faced with her own seems to be an insurmountable obstacle – DJ rose above it all.

The Storm Carriers

DJ was like the four storm carriers in Mark 2 (ESV) who loved their paralyzed friend enough to defy conventional means to get him needed help. In Verse 4 it says, "And when they could not get near Him because of the crowd, they removed the roof above Him, and when they had made an opening, they let down the bed on which the paralytic lay."

Because of their faith, Jesus healed that man. Like that paralyzed man, my sister and I could not lift ourselves, yet DJ's love and kindness lifted us. That generous moment gave us refuge in a strange place and subsequently the strength we needed to continue through the fight.

This was love in action. As it says in Romans 15:1 (ESV), "We who are strong have an obligation to bear with the failings of the weak, and not to please ourselves." DJ's dinner showed how we can make the difference in the life of another through a simple act of kindness.

Step Out on Faith

About 24 hours after DJ blessed us, on my 6th day in the hospital, there was a significant shift in my condition. Things were looking better. I had gotten significantly better, but life as I knew it would not be the same. Along with the diagnosis of pneumonia, the doctors found ulcerative colitis, a chronic disease that affects the colon and rectum, together known as the large intestine. The innermost lining of the large intestine becomes inflamed. Ulcers, which are tiny open sores, can form on the surface. I call it the fraternal twin to Crohn's disease since they share some of the same symptoms but are treated differently.

They explained to me that it is an incurable condition. Well, I had plans of living a very long time, but life with UC was not a part of that plan. Let me paint a picture of how that would play out in my everyday life.

As an elder in the Lord's church, musician, professional trainer, instructional designer, project manager, and orator, a part of my job involves travel throughout the United States and abroad. During what I call the "high tide" of this diagnosis, imagine having to deliver a training session, lecture, or minister before a crowd that can range to thousands at a time and constantly having strong, immediate urges to use the bathroom. So, you are compelled to add an unplanned break to the schedule or leave the class or session only to discover – false alarm!

Imagine being at the airport and about to board a plane. All of a sudden, you get the urge to go again, and this time it's for real, or so you think.

Do you get out of line and handle your business?

Do you explain to the airline assistants what's going on with you?

Do you get on the plane and take care of the matter on the plane?

Let's say you choose the latter. The pilot announces, "Ladies and Gentlemen, the seat belt sign is on; please, remain in your seats until the seat belt light is turned off." And, as the last few words fall off the pilot's lips, you get that urge to go again. You're waiting for that light to go off, and the pilot announces, "Ladies and Gentlemen, we are experiencing turbulence. Please, remain seated with your seat belts fastened a while longer."

To say the least – Not good! PainFULL! Depressing! Scary! StressFULL! Embarrassing! All of the above combined is the best description of the agony associated with the condition.

Let's take it a step farther. On Sunday or your primary day of worship, you get dressed for church. Just before you walk out the door of your home, "Urge-to-Go" shows up. You work your way through that moment. You are driving and have learned not to stop for coffee and donuts any longer. You see, with UC, you must calculate your every move. It's almost like timing contractions for a pregnant woman. Finally, you get to church and thank God there were no traffic delays, that you did not get pulled over or were not involved in an accident, and just as you open the door to enter the sanctuary, "Urge-to-Go" shows up again. You make a U-turn to handle your business. Oops! It was another false alarm.

So, you are frustratingly happy that it was indeed a false alarm. You enter the sanctuary but choose to sit toward the back so that you can get to the bathroom in a non-intrusive way just in case. Being a leader and expected to sit toward the front so that you are readily available to assist on demand, you struggle internally because you want to do what is required of you, but because of this thing, you must sit toward the back of the church. After a while, you've had enough of trying to explain your condition and actions you take to manage the condition. Trying to compromise, you move in closer and twitch in your seat trying to control your nerves and "Urge-to-Go." With ulcerative colitis, even with medication, one must respond to *every* urge. One never knows whether or not the outcome will be a false alarm.

DJ is now in the presence of the Lord, but the impact of her love walk with Christ still lives on in our lives today. Her kindness eased a tempest, but the journey with UC continued. The prospect of the fury that lay ahead left me in prayer for another miracle.

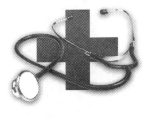

CHAPTER 6

Stuff Happens! Response Makes the Difference

Attitude and response play a major role at the onset of a diagnosis.

Will you lie down, roll over, and just accept The Enemy's invitation to possess sickness that he offers through symptoms? Or, will you call his bluff and choose to trust what God has said – we are already healed. God has provided for our well-being even before you and I would ever experience sickness. It is critically important to choose right in the moment of diagnosis that in spite of what the diagnosis may be, you will rely on God's promise for healing in your mind, body, and soul. It is what you decide in *that* moment that lays the foundation and sets the course for success through the entire journey.

What will be *your* stance? Will you trust Him? Can you see yourself coming through the situation completely whole? Will you buckle to negative thoughts that flood your mind?

Once your stance is determined, you must not waiver. If you falter, the momentum of your faith is interrupted. Once it is interrupted, you might not be able to regroup and rebuild it in time to get the results you need. Ultimately, you might lose the ability to fight altogether. That is the toll sickness and disease take on people. It saps the life and strength to fight out of us.

Anatomical texts indicate that the human body contains approximately 650 skeletal muscles. If you lift weights, you don't grow muscle number 651. You only expand existing muscles. They are the same muscles just exercised.

Execute your faith like you build your muscles.

STAND ON HIS WORD

As the doctors, nurses, and a nutritionist began to prepare me for going home, they explained life with UC. While they spoke, Holy Spirit adlibbed in my inner ear, "Decide right now what your response and stance are going to be in spite of what they are telling you."

The medical team stressed that I'd have to drastically change my diet…good-bye to cookies, candy bars, and a bag of chips. I had to let it all go and then some!

Before UC, I could eat what I wanted, when I wanted it, and how much of it I wanted. It was nothing for me to eat a full meal in the midnight hour and not experience any kind of reaction. Candies! Cookies! Cakes! Ice cream! Mexican! Italian! Soul food! Spicy or mild! I could eat it all and have no problems.

With UC, all of this changed. (I'll tell you in depth in Chapter 7 what living with UC is really like.) How my body responded to what I ate became extremely unpredictable. I lived in constant, threatening fear of what foods and drinks I consumed. At times, I negotiated with myself as to whether or not I'd drink a glass of water, a shot of water, or none at all. As harmless as it seemed, I never knew how my excretory system would respond.

Will the water stay down? Will it cause my bowels to suddenly move without control? I just did not know what would happen.

When I was out and about with friends and we stopped for food, I was very hesitant to order anything other than soup and crackers – soup without all the trimmings and more like bullion. I only ate full, solid meals if I was in the privacy of my own home and maybe in the homes of a few trusted friends who knew my dilemma. This helped to minimize being embarrassed about staying in the bathroom too long or wondering what people thought if I flushed the toilet several times because I thought I'd finished emptying out only to discover a minute later that I still needed to go.

So, I heard what the medical team said, but at the same time I heard what Holy Spirit spoke to me through the scriptures. It was a still, quiet Voice, but the impact was as strong as someone using a bullhorn to speak directly into my ear. The Voice overshadowed the sound of any negative thought that tried to rise up. The Voice silenced the "You'll-never-beat-this" that tried to root and ground itself in my mind. He, the Voice, was doing His job – to bring all things to my remembrance, whatsoever God has said to me (John 14:26). God said that I was already healed according to Isaiah 53:5. The Voice reminded me of this.

If there was ever a time I needed this to be true, the time was now. I put the God of the Bible verses that dealt with the promise of healing on trial. Preachers and Bible teachers had told me all my life that "God is not a man, that he should lie, or a son of man, that he should change his mind. Has he said, and will he not do it? Or has he spoken and will he not fulfill it" (Numbers 23:19 ESV)? I took them at His word.

Either His word is true, or it is not was my resolve. I was willing to stand on His word whether or not I beat UC and lived or died. I had no fear of death. It is what helped me to draw a line in the sand. I relied on Isaiah 53:5 the most: "But He was wounded for our transgressions, he was bruised for our iniquities; the chastisement of our peace was upon him; and with his stripes we are healed."

I personalized the latter portion of that verse and rehearsed it every day all day long. I went to sleep reciting "…with his stripes I am healed." I woke up reciting "…with his stripes I am healed." I recited this passage inwardly throughout the day. When the negative voices attempted to raise their volume in my ear to convince me otherwise, I boldly exclaimed the passage aloud as if The Enemy and I were standing face to face in a shout out battle.

"The doctors say UC is incurable…you've got to live with it the rest of your life…take the meds or else…," he said.

As The Enemy tried to smooth talk me, I heard Holy Spirit say, "Remember, 'submit yourselves therefore to God. Resist the devil, and he will flee from you'" (James 4:7). He asked, "Didn't you do this already?"

I had done this. This time I simply told The Enemy, "Go!" He quickly left.

WORD OF MOUTH

Holy Spirit did His job. He brought God's Word to my remembrance. I was on track with adding my part to the equation. I practiced what I'd begun to learn when I was a very young girl.

From age 6 to 13, I attended Immaculate Conception Elementary School (IC) in Clarksdale, Mississippi. This is one of the places where my interest in God and the scriptures began. As students at IC, we were required to attend mass on a weekly basis, whether we were Catholic or not. It was part of the curriculum. Each week, a different student was afforded the opportunity to do a scripture reading before other students, faculty, and staff. I could hardly wait for my turn. At this time, I had no idea that this would one day be a major part of my salvation and walk with Christ.

My older brothers, Larry, Allen, and I were "classroom Catholics," deeply grateful for the IC education, but we turned to Chapel Hill Missionary Baptist Church, our mom's spiritual home for worship. Week after week and almost never missing a service, we attended the main Sunday services in the morning and an evening Bible training session called Baptist Training Union (BTU). The Bible verses I heard at school were the same ones I heard at church. I'll never forget how my BTU teacher taught us how to find Bible passages (chapter and verse). If my memory serves correctly, John 3:16 was the first verse we had to find and memorize.

She made it interesting by testing us to see who could find the scripture she'd call out first. The reward was sweet treats. Sometimes the verses were very short and easy to learn. At other times passages like the 23rd Psalm or the Lord's Prayer, as recorded in the Gospel of Matthew, were lengthy, but I learned them.

Recitation and writing down the scriptures were key to memorization. Before Post-It Notes became popular, I would write a scripture in the palm of my hands so that I could study it as long as the ink would last throughout the day. Notebook paper was a precious commodity, and my resources were very low. I'd grab a small piece of a brown paper bag and jot down a verse or two to study. I still remember the moment it all clicked for me. How empowered I felt! I excelled at this.

When I approached age 12, Mom decided we would attend my father's church. A part of me was glad about this because I enjoyed the music there, but on the other hand, I did not know if the new church had programs and classes in place that would continue to challenge me to learn the scriptures like at Chapel Hill.

Dad was a member of a Pentecostal church, St. James Temple Church of God in Christ. After the move to St. James, I surprisingly learned a bit more about the Bible as a member of the Sunshine Band, a study group for children 12-years old and younger. It was an experience!

Ninety-nine percent of the scriptures I know today were committed to memory by the time I was 12. Using the learn-by-heart system, we were required to memorize verses from the Bible that began with each letter of the alphabet, except for X and Z. To this day, I refer to them, unlike the list of Old English readings I had to learn in high school. See a copy of the verses list (Appendix A).

When I pull from that list of scriptures, something powerful happens! I take on strength like a smartphone with a dwindling charge, and someone comes along and charges it until the battery is full. I see life more clearly and handle situations with the kind of wisdom only God can give. My confidence increases, and feelings of mental and spiritual lethargy subside. It feels as if I can conquer anything.

ATTITUDE AND RESPONSE

As I stated earlier, attitude and response to adverse situations at the onset are so key to enforcing God's promises concerning our well-being. With that in my heart and mind, and the scriptures embedded in me, exchanges about living with ulcerative colitis on a lifelong basis were the furthest from my mind. I had *no* intentions of living with those experiences the rest of my life. Here is where the battle of the mind escalated to a rather heated inner exchange between my talk with God and what my mind was giving voice to in light of what the doctors said.

Things got heated to a degree between members of my medical team and me. They kept referring to my bout with UC as, "your disease," or "your ulcerative colitis." You hear it on commercials all the time when certain medical advertisements come on – "your restless leg syndrome," "your diabetes," or "your whatever." Hearing my doctor and others on my medical team use the words, "your disease," bothered me. It seemed as if it was The Enemy's subtle approach to persuade me to accept their possible, suggested conclusions as my ultimate fate.

It bothered me so much that I asked the doctors, nurses, and nutritionist to stop using that language with me. When I expressed this to them, they'd go into a brief lecture about how I needed to accept this as my truth and not ignore the problem. But, I was not ignoring the problem. I was actively denying UC permission to exist in my body.

The doctors finally got the pneumonia under control. They were able to remove the fluid from my lungs. My excretory system responded to the medications. My bowels were under control. The urge to go was back to normal. My blood pressure was normal, and with medication stayed within the range of 120/80. My temperature was back to 98.6. My heart rate was no longer racing and consistently remained within the range of 60 and 100 beats per second in a rested state. I was able to walk again without assistance. I was a happy camper, almost the old me, but not thrilled that this thing was going home with me!

A LONG WALK HOME

The medical staff prepared me to go home. It was like going back to school in so many ways. I was on a schedule around the clock to learn how to cope with this disease at home. As the nurses would give me my meds, they explained what I should take, how often to take them, what side effects to look out for, what to do if any occurred, and what to do if I missed a dosage.

I met with a nutritionist to learn about what I should and should not eat. She gave me forms that were to help me track the food I ate and reactions to the food if any occurred. She drilled the importance of proper meal planning and advanced preparation. Failure to do both would increase the odds of eating from fast food restaurants, which she strongly suggested I avoid. She was right! Both worked together to maintain a healthy diet in general and to help control UC.

With members of the medical team coming in and out of my room around the clock, I did not get much rest or sleep and resorted to watching television or talking on the telephone to my siblings. Rerun after rerun, conversation after conversation, sleep was nowhere to be found. However, a few days into the preparation for going home, my upswing took a downturn. I caught a fresh cold!

I was not about to let the common cold delay my trip home, so I worked very hard to get rid of it. I applied the Word of God, "...with His stripes I am healed." I rehearsed this over and over again until my mind, body, and The Enemy got the message from what was in my heart and the words that came out of my mouth.

I challenged The Enemy: "If you want to hear me call on the Name of Jesus, the Name that is above every other name, the Name the righteous call on to find safety, the Name that already defeated you, then bring on the new symptoms."

That cold went away within a day!

To see the situation change right before my eyes did me good. It expanded my faith muscles and assured me that everything would be alright. It was just a matter of time.

Many pray, "Lord, increase my faith," when He has already given us all the faith we will ever have – it's called *"the* measure," not *"a* measure." All we need to do is use what we have.

When we use our faith without wavering and start to see the desired results, it seems as if one has been dealt additional faith, or the power of faith is increased. Faith expands as a result of usage and when you mix it with the Word (Hebrews 4:2). To mix the Word with faith is a decision to accept what you have heard as truth and to expect it to happen. The Word says we were and are healed. Then, we are healed in spite of what we see, think, or feel. However, to actualize it, we must follow the prescription.

The task is to set the mind to agree with what has been spoken. And, with the agreement, we show some outward sign that reflects that decision. That's called corresponding action. We simply ask Holy Spirit to tell us what that translates into, and do just what He says. That is how we mix the Word with faith.

Now, turn on your mixer!

CHAPTER 7

Home, Sweet Home!

On the eighth day of my hospital stay, my medical team started to talk to me about the possibility of going home. I can't describe how excited this made me feel. But, with this, the doctor forewarned that going home was contingent upon consistent normal readings of my vital signs. So, I had to play the waiting game.

Then something good happened! On Day 11, the doctor informed me that I could go home the next day if all my levels remained stable throughout that night.

Finally, the day for me to go home arrived – Day 12. Earline had packed my clothes and gathered my toiletries, and all my cards and flowers. I sat fully dressed, and as close as possible to the door of my hospital room. I waited and waited. In the meantime, I daydreamed about walking into my house after almost two weeks. I could see myself entering the house and rushing to say hello to my fish (all fifty-five of them). They were freshwater fish of many vibrant colors and various sizes. I had visions of soaking in my bath tub since I had not been able to use one for twelve days.

Lunchtime rolled around. I wasn't sure if I should place my order especially if it would delay me from going home.

Worst-case scenario, I'll take a doggie bag, I thought to myself. So, I placed my order.

Lunch arrived within the hour. *What was keeping him?* I began to wonder more aggressively because the doctor still had not come to give the final word. *Was I going home today or not?*

My sister tried to keep me calm. We talked about grocery shopping and the things she'd like to look for when we could really go out without fear of either one of us getting too tired. The medical staff kept me somewhat occupied. They checked my temperature, blood pressure, heart rate, and sugar levels several times, and continued to give me meds on schedule. All was within normal range. Great news!

FREE AT LAST

Around 3 p.m. that day in August 2006, my physician finally showed up. His first words to me were, "Looks like somebody is ready to go home." We all chuckled. I was beyond ready.

He reviewed my charts and nodded his head in an assuring, affirmative manner. He placed the stethoscope on my stomach. I was always curious why he had done this and finally was alert enough to ask why.

"This allows me to listen to the abdominal sounds your intestines make," he said. "If I hear little to no activity, I'd have to check out why things are so quiet. You just ate lunch, so I should be hearing something going on in there. The rumbling I heard means the situation is very good. Your gastrointestinal tract is working as it should."

I asked him if I could listen, too. He cleaned the stethoscope and placed them on my ears. I felt like a little child exploring with the doctor's tools.

As I listened to my insides, I smiled at my sister and then my doctor with a shocked look on my face. I was in awe at what sounded like a river rushing through pipes all inside of me. Thoughts of Jonah inside the whale that swallowed him flashed through my mind. Then, I gave out an extended "Wowwwwwww!" This was as articulate as I could be in that moment.

They laughed. As the doctor reached for the stethoscope, he smiled.

"You are going home today!" he said. "The nurses will stop by with final instructions for you, check you out, and escort you to your car."

The ride home was pretty quiet. There I was riding along as a passenger, inwardly thinking, which led to inwardly thanking God for sparing my life. Everything looked different. Trees were in the middle of transitioning from summer to fall. The leaves were redder than red, greener than green, and golder than gold. The sound of traffic and watching cars come and go was thrilling.

On any other day before this ordeal, I'd wish the car in front would speed up and hope the driver behind could comprehend that my flashing signal light really meant that I was about to turn. Seldom riding in the passenger seat, I soaked in the scenery from this point of view – a view that allowed me to see all that I'd missed when I was well and drove myself and all that I'd missed because I was in the hospital those twelve days.

Finally, we made it to the house. What a joy!

Back to the Familiar

I could see my fish again. I was happy. In a matter of time, I'd take a soak in my tub, sleep in my own bed, wallow on my couch, get a cold drink from my own refrigerator, take a shower in my own shower, and put on clothes that were not open in the back. What a joy!

As I eased into the rest of the day, recovering from my experiences was still in full effect. Thoughts about things I had to catch up on bombarded my mind. I contacted my job to let them know that I was home and to give an estimate for my return. Laundry, groceries, and vacuuming tasks were next in line. As much as I wanted to immediately dive into those tasks, I had to wait. I was still under the influence of a host of medications that made me a little drowsy. So, household chores and driving were out of the question.

After bringing in the luggage and the flowers that my friends had given me, my sister and I decided to go our separate ways in the house. Left alone to rest or do whatever I wanted to do, thoughts about living with UC came to mind.

Would my body start to reject the medication after so long? I wondered. *What would happen if I missed a dose or stop taking it altogether? After all, the gastroenterologist told me, I'd have to take this medication the rest of my life.*

Just how long is the rest of my life? The thoughts went on. *How long would it be before I feel like my old self again?*

After thinking for a few hours, I got hungry. Instead of asking Earline to prepare something for me, I took it upon myself to give cooking a try. In an attempt to rationalize this decision, inwardly I thought, *I need to get back on my feet as quickly as possible. Now is the time to get started.*

Earline must have heard me in the kitchen because she came down about five minutes later.

There I stood looking in the cupboard with a blank stare, and just as Earline made her way down the stairs and walked into the kitchen, I started tossing things into the trash. She came closer toward me and asked in a firm kind of a way, *"What are you doing?"*

"I've got to get rid of this stuff because it is not on my new diet sheet," I explained.

Stuff! she exclaimed. "You are throwing away things I just bought! You're putting money in the garbage!"

"Oh! My!" I stated in a mildly sarcastic way. "I didn't know you went to the grocery store. Soooooo, you learned the area well enough to do that on your own."

"Don't forget," she said jokingly but with a very serious look on her face. "I was traveling before you were born."

I apologized profusely.

We continued to talk a little while longer – thirty minutes or so as she prepared dinner. Without any notion that this was about to occur, she looked at me, and I looked at her – we locked eyes and began to laugh uncontrollably at the same time. Neither one of us needed to say anything – not one word. It was understood from this point on that she would manage the kitchen and meals for the duration of her stay.

"LOLO" TO THE RESCUE

Another week passed, and the time came for this particular sister to go home. RB, another one of my storm carriers, stood in the gap and stayed with me until my sister Delores arrived a day later.

"Lolo," as I affectionately called her, was the eighth of 13 children in our family.

When I grew up, she was the eldest in the house. She was the one who combed my hair and dressed me before she left for school. When she left the house to walk to school with her friends, I sneaked out of the house every chance I got and followed her until a neighbor or another family member let her know.

When I started first grade, she was my savior. There were many days

I left home without money to buy lunch. Whether we had money or not, we went to school. I was blessed because for every single day I left home without lunch money, LoLo showed up at lunch time with something for me to eat. If she was unable to provide lunch or money to buy food, she escorted me home and scrounged up something. She grew to become an amazing woman, with the gift of creating something out of little to no resources.

Delores arrived. The cook of cooks among us girls, she cooked breakfast, lunch, dinner, and prepared healthy snacks in between...I'll always love, appreciate, and remember her unselfish acts.

I slowly acclimated myself to driving again. Managing my house and affairs was easier, but I still had to take it easy.

Here is what learning to take it easy entailed:

1. I learned to say NO to a lot of extracurricular activities and replaced that time with plenty of scheduled, deliberate rest.
2. I drastically changed my diet and stopped eating junk food throughout the day.
3. I started a journal, recording how my body responded when I ate certain foods.
4. I did extensive research online until I found a food set and dietary and exercise regimen that worked for me. Here's a list of what I eliminated:

   • Bread – wheat in particular. If I consumed it, it had to be burnt toast...the charcoal effect of the bread in this form seemed to digest very well for me. I wasn't genius enough to come up with this idea but found it as I read the success stories of others who experienced the same or a similar life trauma.
   • Whole milk. Making the switch to almond milk was easy because I primarily used it when I ate cereal, and that wasn't often.
   • Refined sugar. The white stuff in the box or bag hasn't proven to be good for the human body and had such addictive, adverse effect on me. After viewing pictures of the amount

of sugar used in a single soft drink alone, letting it go was a no-brainer. Soda or soft drinks became a definite no-no for me. If I consumed it, it certainly was not on a regular basis. In exchange for white sugar, Sugar in the Raw (cane sugar) became my sweetener of choice.

- Equal. This and other unnatural sugar substitutes were on the do-not-touch-ever-again list.
- Enriched flour. Tough to eliminate because it is found in so many dry baked goods (donuts, cake, and especially cookies), and when it came to cookies, you could just call me Cookie Monster like the Sesame Street character – "Me loves cookies!" As I learned about the alternatives, I could more easily make the switch.
- Aspartame. My research indicated that this is a chemical found in embalming fluid – enough said!
- Fried foods – chicken, fish, french fries.

I said goodbye to my cookies, donuts, potato chips, candy bars, ice cream, white rice, shrimp, pork, red meats, and processed foods in general until I was convinced that I'd reset my body. Thereafter, my goal was to consume in moderation.

Those were all of my favorites that I learned to live without…initially, I went cold turkey on eliminating those foods. That caused my body to be in a love-hate relationship with me, but my health was improving. Bloating was now a thing of the past because I stopped drinking sodas. I was able to control when I went to the bathroom. As long as I remained loyal to the food regimen and took my meds, my bodily functions remained in check. In spite of the progress, my mind and body were at odds over those good-to-me foods.

Unless I cheated a little, which was rarely during the body reset process, the new diet included:

- Almonds
- Baked chicken
- Brown Rice
- Cabbage

- Collards
- Eggs
- Fruit
- Green Beans
- Grits
- Honey or Sugar in the Raw (later replaced with Xylitol)
- Kale
- Lamb
- Oatmeal
- Pinto Beans
- Salmon
- Sunflower seeds
- Turkey or chicken breasts
- Walnuts
- Yams
- Yogurt

For three straight months, I learned to live without my goodies. The change in diet helped tremendously, but evidence that the root cause of the problem still lurked showed up from time to time. Every four to six weeks, I experienced mildly explosive bowel movements and rectal bleeding.

Was this The Enemy's attempt to get me to change my confession? Is this as good as it will ever get for me? I thought.

All I had to say to this was, "NOT!"

Power in the Blood

Every time a symptom showed up, and as quickly as fear tried to set in, the declarations I mentioned earlier instantly stood up in me as if the Word was on autopilot. It was as if Holy Spirit fed me my lines as I encountered each symptom.

"Speak to the root cause, fear, and each symptom," I heard Him say. "Tell them there is still power in the blood; and, it still works. With His stripes you are healed. 'No weapon formed against you shall prosper'" (Isaiah 54:17).

"There is still power in the blood and the Name of Jesus" I told those symptoms. "Body you are already healed. Now act like it!"

Within a day, all symptoms left and stayed away for several months at a time. The gap was longer and longer between each subsequent flare-up. However, the bowel problems showed up from time to time to see if I was serious about my confession.

Ain't nothing changed, I told them in my thoughts. *I'm still healed in spite of what I see, think, or feel.*

Enforcing the Word of God works!

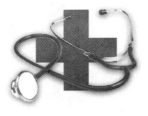

CHAPTER 8

The Memo!

While life for me was getting back to normal, and the very expensive medications were doing what they were supposed to do, I was not at peace with myself.

In 2006, a 30-day supply of Asacol cost $267.65, the most expensive of all my prescriptions. Today, the replacement drug, Asacol HD, costs $1400 for 180 tablets. That was one of ten or more different prescription medicines I took every day. Each had extreme possible side effects when taken for an extended period of time. I kept my follow-up appointments, and with every visit, I'd ask my doctor when he was going to reduce the dosages or stop the medications.

Now, don't get me wrong. I am thankful that the medications were instrumental in stabilizing my condition. But, something about taking them forever didn't agree with me. So, finally after about nine months of follow-up medical appointments, I stated emphatically to my medical team that I wanted to reduce the drugs and monitor how my body would respond. I needed to know if without the medication, I could live without the symptoms.

My primary gastroenterologist told me that if he changed or stopped the medications, I would have a setback. If he were to alter the medications and dosages, the condition would re-emerge with a vengeance. If that were the case, and the need arose for me to start the medications again, the bottom line was there would be no guarantee that the medication would work again.

So, at what would become my final appointment with the lead gastroenterologist, I expressed my feelings again. He replied, "If you can't take the medicine the way I prescribe it, then you'll have to find yourself another doctor."

I replied, "You couldn't have given me a better option."

I remember this exchange as if it were yesterday! This occurred near Memorial Day weekend of 2006. On that day, I stood in my kitchen pondering some things in my heart. I was talking out aloud to God, as I often do.

"God, I feel like a hypocrite taking this medication," I said. "Your Word says that healing is the children's bread – my body is hungry for healing. The doctors said I have to be on this medication the rest of my life. That doesn't align with what You say I can have."

In the ear of my heart I heard Him speak, "The ball is in your court, Jackie. Whatever you decide, I'll back you up."

I believed my body was healed. At that moment in time, I was reminded about a woman the Bible speaks of – the woman with the issue of blood. She suffered with this issue for 12 long years.

Jesus was preaching and was surrounded by a multitude of people. While in the press, that woman touched the hem of His garment. Jesus paused and asked, "Who touched me?"

Shocked at the question, the disciples replied in essence: "All of these people out here and you ask who touched you?"

Clearly, they were operating with their natural senses. Jesus wanted to know who had touched the very essence of His being, the God part of Him. In the end, the woman was healed.

"I didn't heal you," He told her. "It was your faith that has made you whole."

Right then, I took a stand, and decided to stop the medications cold turkey. I succumbed to fear only one time after that decision. I saw blood one day and took the pills. I pulled myself together the next day, however, and did a redirect of my faith. I decided in that moment, sink or swim, live or die, I will stand on the Word, even if it costs me my life.

So, am I saying it's wrong to take medication?

Absolutely not! Do what you have to do to stay alive.

Faith told me that it had looked over into God's provision for healing. If I wanted it, it was mine. Not taking the medications was my God-assigned corresponding action - "faith without works is dead" (James

2:26). Your corresponding action may be different. Whatever it is, be sure He is speaking to you.

As time continued to pass, I saw less and less of the symptoms that resulted in my 12-day hospital stay. Little things crept up, but I remained steadfast in my faith and declarations.

In one case, a lump about the size of a marble appeared on my right hand out of nowhere and for no apparent reason. Though it did not cause any pain, it was an annoyance.

Still functioning with that constant "urgent need to go," I continued to do domestic travel for work and ministry, and then the ultimate test arose.

In March of 2010, I was asked to go to Tel Aviv, Israel to conduct a global technical training session for my employer. The company was putting on a conference there and would pay my airfare and all expenses. I was selected to participate because I was the only one in the organization that trained customers on a particular proprietary software program.

Imagine flying from the United States to Israel. That's a 16-hour trip at a minimum! Occasional symptoms, no medication, and the big question of whether or not I should take the trip clouded my thoughts.

As before, I stood on the promise of God and decided to take the trip. Nothing was going to keep me off that plane.

CHAPTER 9

True to His Word

That nine-day trip was amazing! Not one symptom manifested.

While there, and as I'll explain later, I attended a lecture on the Dead Sea Scrolls, and celebrated Purim, a Jewish festival that commemorates the defeat of Haman who plotted a massacre of the Jews as recorded in the book of Esther. I ate and drank what I wanted with my colleagues, who truly understand the significance of that celebration.

I finished my work for the conference, and I was super excited because I wasn't sure if I could even make a trip of this magnitude given what I'd experienced in the past four years. All I could do was thank God for all the blessings. He allowed me to take an all-expense paid trip to the Holy Land.

God kept all the symptoms and discomforts associated with ulcerative colitis from me – no stomach pain, no bleeding, and no immediate urges to use the bathroom constantly throughout the day. My thoughts were filled with praise. At the same time, I prayed that I could remain in good health for the three additional days I was to remain in Israel – one day in Tel Aviv, and two days in Jerusalem.

The purpose of the extended stay was for me to meet staff at headquarters. These were people I'd worked with over the phone but had never seen. It's always nice to be able to put a face with a name and voice!

Although my stay was extended for work purposes, I had the weekend to myself but had not given thought to how I would fully spend that time. Then, I thought to myself that I could not possibly leave the wonderful cities of Tel Aviv and Jerusalem and not walk where Jesus walked and pray where He prayed. Opportunities like this do not always repeat themselves! So, I took advantage of this one.

We were staying in Tel Aviv. One of my colleagues, LF, and I impulsively decided to unwind from the intensity of the conference and after-conference activities. Operating on adrenaline, we decided to go walking. If we had taken the time to change clothes, order food, and eat right then, we probably would have succumbed to our exhaustion and might have abandoned the idea of getting away from the conference scene.

As we made our split-second decision, we agreed to leave our training materials and computers in our rooms and immediately head out just as we were. We did not know how far we might go. LF was seven months pregnant. I was sleep deprived because I could not get used to the eight-hour time difference. Most nights I wrestled the sheets and pined for my bed back in the States. The interesting thing with all this is that LF seemed to have more energy than I had.

The Charles Clore Park was opposite our hotel, the Dan Panorama. We walked along this park, on the banks of the Mediterranean Sea. The wind blew as if its goal was to clean the earth in one, fell swoop. The breezes off the waves felt chilly, but nothing compared with what I might face in a stroll that time of year along Lake Michigan. I never imagined how over 2,000 years since the time of Christ, the area would look so ordinary.

The Footsteps of Jesus

It was a typical beach front. Children ran. They played what appeared to be kickball. People laughed, swam, and did what might be seen of a beach in California, New York, or Florida. There was no sign of the sacred except in one experience we witnessed.

Some children called out saying, "Abba, Abba!" They were yelling, "Father" with such joy on their faces. They ran and jumped into their fathers' arms at full speed. The fathers smiled or laughed as they caught them and gave them warm hugs and kisses. Hearing the children call their fathers "Abba" touched my soul and brought tears to my eyes. It reminded me of how much I miss my natural father. Whenever I was in my dad's presence, he didn't say much, but he always gave me his golden smile. That spoke volumes to me. He loved me unconditionally. He provided for me. He took good care of me. It also reminded me of the relationship I have with my heavenly Father – I call Him Abba, too! He takes good care of me. He provides for me. He loves me unconditionally. And, here I was in the land where it all began.

As we walked, those thoughts left me in the face of something I find hard to love. The dogs were not on leashes for the most part, and that caused me to be very uncomfortable to say the least. Whenever we would pass someone walking a dog, I moved as far away from the path of the animal as I could without alarming the dog. Yes, I left the pregnant woman who loves dogs closer to the path of the four-legged friends that came our way.

Sea gulls flew overhead and sometimes too low in my opinion. Yep, I dodged them just in case they decided to relieve themselves over my head. While running to avoid them, I laughed and said to my colleague, "I am really not an outdoor person."

She laughed so hard at me, and said, "I see!"

The birds appeared to talk to one another and made periodic landings along the beach. We watched as they attempted to catch fish from the sea. Some were successful and others not as successful.

The boisterous waves roared, rolled, and clashed against the bank of the sea. They appeared to tease us as they retreated within inches of where we stood as if someone commanded them not to come any closer. God was good.

If I did not already believe in God, I would surely be on the verge of believing because my little mind could not comprehend the length, breadth, and overall vastness of such a creation that extended way beyond what our eyes were seeing. No man could have created and tamed this mammoth body of water. Only an all-powerful being can command the sea, and have it obey. The waters seemed so immense from the shore, but I was assured that my Lord was the only being who could forbid it to swallow up the earth.

All kinds of thoughts and feelings raced through my mind.

There I stood, where the apostle Paul took many of his missionary journeys by way of the Mediterranean Sea; where the prophet Jonah attempted to flee from God by boarding a ship docked at the Palestinian port of Joppa (Jonah 1:3), which is about 30 miles south of Caesarea. *Is this real?* I thought to myself.

It was fascinating as we watched people from all walks of life, different races, religions, and color go about their day. From a distance, we saw two men in the park that was about seventy-five yards away from the coast. They carried what appeared to be huge, kite-looking objects. As we came closer into the park, we determined that they were paragliders.

Each had one bearing the same bright, florescent-like colors of yellow, red, white, and blue. I don't know if my eyes were playing tricks on me or not. But, the yellow seemed more yellow, the red more red, the white more white, and the blue more blue as the sun rays beamed down on them.

We watched as the guys skillfully set up to take flight. Once everything was in place, they took off running as fast as they could, and the wind took over from there. The wind gradually lifted them higher and higher into the sky as if they were birds. Up, up, and away they went. It was exciting to see. We watched them long enough to land and take off a second time. Then, we moved on.

Since my colleague was scheduled to head back to the States early the next morning, we kept moving so that we could see as much as possible before nightfall and get back to the hotel so that she could rest and prepare for the flight home. We walked about two to three miles more.

We saw individuals fishing with poles and casting nets into the sea. The sight of this made me think about when Jesus recruited His first two disciples. Matthew 4:18 (ESV) states:

> While walking by the Sea of Galilee, he saw two brothers, Simon (who is called Peter) and Andrew his brother, casting a net into the sea, for they were fishermen. And he said to them, "Follow me, and I will make you fishers of men." Immediately they left their nets and followed him.

Beyond that, the experience brought back memories of the times when my brother-in-law, PJ, took me fishing in the Adirondacks near Upstate New York. He had a small cabin and a boat there. It was his own little piece of paradise, which he so freely shared with family and friends. Seeing the Israeli locals fish and thinking about PJ was all so surreal. Fact and imagination became one in that moment.

As we approached the two-hour mark into our walk, suddenly an unusual sound of music filled the air and seemed to be broadcast over the entire city of Tel Aviv. As far as we walked, it continued to play. Aside from hearing this sound on television while watching movies based in the Middle East, it was foreign to me. I looked at my colleague and asked,

"Why is that strange music broadcasting over this entire area?

"It's not just music; it's a call to prayer and worship for those who practice Islam," she explained.

In one instance I see individuals responding to this call with no hesitation whatsoever. Then, I recall, how I saw priests on the flight to Israel and others of the Jewish faith stop in their tracks wherever they were, face east, and they prayed. It did not matter who was looking on or what others thought or said.

There is no shame to their game. I thought.

I couldn't help but to think about how I might be shy to be that public with my devotion. Something in me changed.

It seemed as if someone pressed a "Play" button in my mind and showed me the times when I was reluctant to express my faith in the marketplace. I was ashamed of myself for failing to sometimes give thanks or pray in public. I watched the Arab worshipers and considered Matthew 10:33. Christ says, "… whoever shall deny me before men, him will I also deny before My father which is in heaven."

Typically, if I were out shopping and encountered someone, and in our exchange that person asked me to pray for them, I'd commit to praying for them but later. After this experience, when asked to pray, I pray in the moment.

Time was winding down. We increased our pace and set out to purchase some items to take home to family and friends. We finally arrived to an area where the shops ranged from shanties to the kind of modern buildings very similar to those in the States. Souvenir options seemed to be within every 50 steps or less. Several of the store operators would call out to us or beckon for us to pay their shops a visit. We responded to some as a courtesy. We purchased items from others.

Depending on whom you talked to and your negotiation skills, you could walk away having paid less than the asking price. We did! I bought t-shirts and jewelry for my siblings and close friends. I purchased tallits (a fringed garment) for some of my preacher friends. And, of course, I purchased a few items for myself.

There were outdoor food stands and restaurants everywhere. Oh! How good the food smelled. It was calling my name. But, just as it was calling my name, fear tried to set in, too – fear of how my body would respond if I were to try the different food options in the courtyard. This was one of the few times this occurred while I was in Israel. In that moment, I whispered, "With your stripes I am healed."

For a few moments fear created a short delay, but as quickly as it came, it left. I bought a hot dog, ate it, and had nooooooo problems.

Nighttime was rapidly approaching and getting back to the hotel before dark was next on our list. Our coastline tour needed to end. That was OK because we had accomplished our goal of seeing a little of Tel Aviv and not going home empty handed – we both wanted to bring a piece of Israel home to our families and friends. So, we headed back to the hotel.

For a minute I thought we would have to hail a taxi because I was getting tired. The adrenaline rush was fading. After about 4 hours of walking, we finally made it back to the hotel. With lots of smiles and laughter, we recapped our day of exploration. As we were about to go our separate ways, my colleague inquired about what I was going to do the rest of the weekend since Israel shuts down to observe Sabbath, and I would be in Israel until Monday.

"I have one tour scheduled for Sunday. Saturday, I'll just hang out in my room," I said.

"Why don't you schedule a few more tours? I did a tour of the Dead Sea and Masada. I think you will find them very interesting," she said. "And, they offer tours on Saturday."

I'll strongly consider it," I said with strong intent.

We embraced and went our separate ways.

Exhausted but in a good way, I was so glad to get back to my room. In spite of being tired and hungry again, I called my sisters (Earline, Bonnie, Cookie, Betty, Sue, and Delores) and five friends (Evelyn, Gloria, Gwen, Princeola, and Tracy) to tell them about my day. I walked them through every step we took using the pictures I'd captured as a guide. Costs for each call was nowhere on my mind until I got home to the surprise of my life – an approximate $2,000 phone bill! I must have talked to each of them thirty minutes to an hour each.

After finishing the last call home, I scheduled my Saturday tours.

My body was now screaming, *Go to sleep!* My mind said, *Don't go to sleep; go online and get familiar with the areas you'll see tomorrow. Make sure you confirm phone numbers to the American Embassy.*

I gave in to the brochures. Saturday morning 8 a.m. Israel Standard Time came faster than I'd imagined. I was so excited about what was ahead that I did not get much sleep during the night.

STAND OF THE FAITHFUL

My first scheduled commercial tour was a two-for- the-price-of-one kind of a deal. It included a visit to Masada and the Dead Sea. Now amazed at having walked the coastline of the Mediterranean Sea and becoming somewhat familiar with its Biblical history, I desired more and more to at least lay eyes on the Dead Sea.

I'd heard that regular use of the Dead Sea salt could help improve many things that ail the body – things like psoriasis, arthritis, dry skin, eczema, stress, insomnia, muscular aches, and skin allergies – my goal was simple – I just wanted to see and stand in it. If it impacted my body in any way, shape, or form, that was OK with me.

I could hardly wait for this tour to kick off as evidenced by being dressed and ready to go by 6 a.m. – departure time was 8 a.m. The bus arrived on time, we did a roll-check and were on our way. What was ahead was about a two-hour drive to Masada. We would stop at the Dead Sea on the way back, which is about an hour from Jerusalem.

The smooth ride of the bus made sleep irresistible. About thirty minutes into the ride, many had fallen asleep. I did all I could to stay awake. From the looks of it, others had the same problem. I saw heads bobbing and weaving, and it wasn't because we were having a rocky ride. We were falling in and out of sleep as others quietly rode along.

Just as the sleep was about to get really good, the bus started to slow down. That abruptly awakened me. As I started to open my eyes and began to look around, I saw men dressed in military uniforms and carrying weapons. One of them signaled for the driver to stop the bus. I wondered, *Can anyone hear the drum beat of my heart as it pounds in my chest?* I said to myself, "Jackie, inhale and slowly exhale; fix your face; be cool."

Others on the bus had an inquisitive look on their faces. You could hear whispers from several as they asked one another, "What's going on?" Me? I sat quietly and just observed. OK – I prayed, too!

Jim, our tour guide, put our minds at ease. He announced over the intercom that this was a matter of protocol for us to stop at the security check point. He further explained, "For those of you who have traveled from the United States into Canada, this is a similar process – there's nothing to be afraid of...."

As we moved on, I was quickly drawn back into the scenery. It is what I saw next that I was not prepared to see – camels! Nomads! People living in the desert...tending to their sheep. Images of David who started out taking care of his father's flock before he became king of Israel ambushed my mind. Suddenly, it was as if I were living out a Bible story in real time.

Shortly thereafter, Jim announced we'd arrived at our destination, Masada. He briefly explained the significance of Masada and told us we were about to take a ride we'd probably never taken before. He was right!

Masada runs alongside the Dead Sea and sits 190 feet above sea level. It is about 1,500 feet above the level of the Dead Sea. Driving up to this area seemed harmless. Once you get inside the area, things get a bit interesting when you realize your mode of transportation is to walk up the mountain or ride the cable car – a single cable attached to a big metal box hundreds of feet in the air – no parachute protection!

Our tour guide canvased the group to see if anyone had any medical issues that might be aggravated if we were to walk or ride the cable car. There were no issues revealed, but we all decided we would take the cable car!

As soon as the next available car arrived, everyone in our group as well as other tour groups rushed the car and squeezed on-board like a can of sardines. The view was amazing, but I'll admit it was a little scary. Bodies touching on all sides and face to face within a few inches of one another, we were a little too close for comfort for me. But, I made it.

Once the car started to move, I realized it was way too late to worry about this short inconvenience. I had to put questions about my own sanity and riding the cable car altogether on the back burner. There was no asking of the operator to stop the car and let you out. There was no out except to ride the cable all the way back or walk down the steep mountain trail. We'd come too far to turn around.

In that moment, my mind fast forwarded to the impending journey back down the mountain. *What am I going to do when it is time to leave?* I thought to myself.

Walking down was not going to happen – it would be a journey of several miles, and it was hot. The only thing to do was to go back the same way I came. I knew in my heart of hearts that if I made it down, I'd probably never do this again.

With the ride up the mountain now behind me, I could focus on learning about Masada. Either Jim, our tour guide, was a great historian, or he had been asked every conceivable Masada-based question and had learned his lines well because he had an answer for every question we posed. He made Masada alive again as he walked us through this piece of history. We walked fast to keep up with him and listened closely as he talked.

According to Jim, long after Jesus was born, Zealots revolted against Rome, but their revolt ended in Jerusalem's demise around 70 AD. The Zealots were a group of political adversaries to the Roman government. They were determined to protect their religion and to end Gentile rule of the Jewish people. Survivors of the rebellion fled to Masada, a fortress built by the order of Herod the Great. Herod was the client king of Judea – that is, he was a non-Roman ruler who enjoyed Roman patronage although he was not treated as an equal.

In this revolt, 900 Zealots held out until the Roman army comprised of 15,000 soldiers breached the walls of the fortress. Their attack strategy was to hit at dawn. By the time they struck, the Zealots had ended their lives in suicide in lieu of capture. Hearing this story lead to yet another conviction and challenge for me. I had to ask myself:

> "Am I willing to die for what I believe as the Zealots did? Would I die for the sake of the Gospel of Jesus Christ? Would I endure persecution as Jesus and His disciples did?"

From where I stand today, I'd like to believe the answer to these questions is, "Yes."

I stand on the promise that I am what Paul describes as "heirs of God." He writes, "The Spirit himself bears witness with our spirit that we are the children of God and if children, then heirs—heirs of God and fellow heirs with Christ, provided we suffer with him in order that we may also be glorified with him" (Romans 8:16-17 ESV).

We continued our tour of Herod's former estate. It was fascinating to see that the living back then closely resembles how we live today. The major difference is technology and process improvement over time. The remains of mosaics adorned several walls throughout the fort. There were indoor spas made of stone and mini waterfalls working as faucets. The living quarters for the elite were very spacious with balconies overlooking the mountainous terrain. It was like living in the heavens. It felt as if you could reach out, touch the sky, and grab a piece of a cloud and fashion it into a snow ball.

As we continued to explore the area, I felt like I was Indiana Jones on an archaeological find as Jim pointed out pottery believed to be used by Herod and all who dwelt at Masada. He pointed out structures that were stores, small shops, and the synagogues of old. Everything else was more of the same.

Many began to tire out as the temperature gradually grew warmer and warmer. We decided to make our return and start the drive to the Dead Sea. The Dead Sea was on the route back to our hotel, which was about an hour away.

The Dead Sea resort was comprised of souvenir shops and shops that offered massages with minerals and mud from the Dead Sea. There were restaurants with plenty of good food. We were on our own this time.

Once Jim introduced us to this area, he took us to the actual Dead Sea where if you wanted to swim and wade in the water you could. Finally, he introduced us to our transportation options to and from the shops and sea area.

We could walk or run, or simply enjoy a small train ride back and forth as many times as we desired. So, I rode the train several times until I was ready to confront the water face to face.

By the third time around, I decided to let the train go so that I could begin my exploration of the Dead Sea. I watched as some decided to take mud baths in mud from the Dead Sea. They were hopeful that it would impact them in a special if not miraculous way. I decided I'd just buy some of the mud, take it home, and experiment with it in the privacy of my own home.

The sun was extremely bright and made taking pictures easy. People were swimming and bathing in the sun. Some were throwing and catching Frisbees.

Jim came along and chatted with me for a bit. Just as he was leaving, he said, "You know it is OK to get in the water; you can't drown."

I asked, "How is that possible?"

He explained, "Because of the enormous amount of salt in the water, your body will just float on it."

What he did not say was that if you rolled over to your stomach and were not a good swimmer, you *could* potentially drown from growing tired of holding your neck above the water and eventually having no option but to lower your head face forward into the water – this I learned later and was glad I did not attempt to float in the water. Whether I could swim or not, I was not going to put my entire body in the water – too risky for me being that far from home without any family or friends nearby.

WADE IN THE WATER

I chose to stand at the edge of the land and waited for the waves to roll in on my feet. So, I stood in the Dead Sea. Then, I ran from every wave that had rolled my way – I was not a swimmer and certainly could not drink that much water if something had gone wrong. Jesus did not bid me to come and walk on water as He did Peter. So, I stayed in my lane. The fact remains – I stood in the Dead Sea.

The time for our drive back to Tel Aviv arrived. The ride back was equally as entertaining. We saw more nomads and camels going about their daily routines. I had hoped that we would stop along the way to buy items from little stands that were on the roadside. I thought about this a little longer and decided it was probably not a safe thing to do and quickly dropped that notion. We stayed on schedule, and the driver dropped us off at our respective hotels. My goal for the evening was to pack, order room service, and get some sleep. This time, my body cooperated with this plan.

Sunday rolled around, and this was the day I would enjoy my second commercial tour, a company-sponsored event for conference attendees, and then transition to a hotel in Jerusalem.

Our company headquarters was located in Jerusalem, which is where I was to spend my last day in Israel on-site to meet the rest of the staff.

Our event planner, LG, had arranged for the driver to drop me off at the Dan Boutique Hotel in Jerusalem after the tour. What a relief this was!

When I'd first arrived in Tel Aviv and had to take a taxi to the hotel where the conference was to be held and where I had a reservation, I was most uncomfortable trying to communicate with the driver who only spoke Hebrew but could read English a little – I only spoke English. So, not having to worry about getting from Tel Aviv to Jerusalem (a journey of 33 miles) was a major relief.

Prepared with my luggage and necessities for the day (BlackBerry to take pictures, passport, sun block protection, shades, hat, jacket, bottled water, and snacks), I anxiously waited outside of the hotel for the tour bus to pick me up. The driver was on time. We exchanged pleasantries. As we chatted for a few minutes, he placed my luggage underneath the bus. Then, he signaled that it was OK for me to enter, and I literally hopped onto the bus with a spring in each step that I took. I said my hellos to all who were on the bus and walked quickly but safely to find an available seat.

The reality of what was about to happen heightened my excitement even the more! I was about to walk where Jesus walked!

Then it happened. My feelings started to get the best of me. Happy tears and sad tears both filled my eyes. I was of mixed emotions. I was happy and indeed appreciative for the overall experience. I was also sad for a moment because the reality was that I was doing something major, and my family and close friends were not physically present to share in this experience.

I dared the tears to fall – they totally ignored me and came streaming down, but I caught them before they grabbed the attention of others.

The tour guide took care of some preliminary red tape to ensure everyone scheduled for the tour was on the bus – calling out name after name over the intercom. Then, we were on our way to the old city of Jerusalem.

The ride was an interesting one. Passing through modern day Tel Aviv and then Jerusalem was like driving through a metropolitan area like Chicago or New York City but with worse drivers in my opinion. (I never thought *that* would be possible!). And, to say they drive extremely fast would be an understatement in my opinion. I've seen drivers drive fast, but these drivers seem to push their accelerators to the max!

The architecture was amazing! There were modern buildings, and some of the historical buildings of old still stood bearing great, aesthetic detail. There were olive trees that stood like giants and palm trees that danced in the wind. For the first time in my life, I saw a grapefruit tree and was simply amazed. I'd never seen one before!

We continued our drive to the old city of Jerusalem. Something caught my eye. It was something I'd never seen in the States – members of the military standing with weapons and strategically stationed throughout various areas. Some were male; some were female. They all appeared to be in tiptop condition, and as people engaged them in conversation, they appeared to be very cordial but kept their hands close to the weapons that were strapped to their bodies.

We moved farther into our drive, and I observed more soldiers. By the time I saw this a third time, a little panic tried to accost me. My mind flashed back to September 11th, 2001, when the United States experienced terrorism to a level that it had never experienced before in its history. One minute the Twin Towers in New York City stood tall. In one act of hatred, they were gone taking with them the lives of many innocent people. To this day, I remember exactly what I was doing. I remember being glued to the television for seven straight days waiting and hoping that the authorities would find more people alive. Switching back to that moment, I thought...

I am in Jerusalem among a people that God calls His own, and since I am one of His, too, He'll take good care of me.

I decided I would live in and enjoy the moment without fear. Whatever happens will happen – that was my resolve.

Finally, we entered into the old city of Jerusalem. The driver parked the bus. Before anyone exited, Amnon, the tour guide, reviewed hand signals, safety instructions, and other travel tips to ensure we all stayed together and looked out for one another.

As we all stepped from the bus, it dawned on me that our tour guide had a Biblical name, Amnon. I couldn't dwell on this too much at the time because my breath was taken away as he proceeded to lead us to an area where we could get a panoramic view of the old city.

I was one of the first to get off the bus. Waiting patiently for the others, I glanced over the crowd. There were so many people from so many places. I met a couple of college students that were from Egypt. I asked them what brought them to Israel.

"We just love to travel," was their reply. "It is easy to see a lot of interesting places when you live in the Middle East because many countries are very close, unlike the United States," they explained further.

I continued looking around from where I stood. Then something great happened. I saw someone I knew! Seeing her made me smile really big as she had done whenever I encountered her. It was LG, our event planner extraordinaire. LG lived in Israel. I'd grown fond of her as a person, how she conducted business, and how she so effectively and efficiently communicated. She had a special way of making you feel as if you were worth a million dollars. LG was just a good, good person who loved her family, work, friends, and associates.

LG came up to me with a glowing smile, hugs, and fresh cookies, which I'd grown to love during my short stay in Israel, and t-shirts for us all. As quickly as she appeared, she wished us well and was quickly on her way.

"What just happened," I asked myself. The answer? Something I cannot explain but sure did enjoy.

Full of enthusiasm, Amnon pulled the group together and then climbed on top of a massive rock that elevated him high above the group and pointed out what we would see on this stretch of the tour.

Without any promptings from the group, one of the first things he identified and explained was why the men and women were dressed in fatigues, armed with machine guns and other high-powered weapons. *Was he reading my mind?* I thought.

Amnon proceeded to explain that every one of age in Israel serves in the military. Male or female, you serve and participate in protecting

Israel. I concluded that if I were to encounter any problems while there, almost anyone over the age of 21 could help me – that was comforting. While I was at ease surrounded by security, I still stayed very close to Amnon.

IN THE OLD CITY

We moved on.

Amnon took us to the entry point of the old city, the Tower of David. Numb at the time because it was unbelievable that I was in Israel period, it is only in retrospect that I can somewhat explain what I was feeling. Mom would have been anxious about my being there, but she would've enjoyed receiving a call from me each night as I shared every detail of the day. Dad on the other hand would've said, "Christine, that girl has no business being over there." As far as he was concerned, the only place for me was home with him and Mom. Yep! I was a "daddy's girl."

This tour started to get very real as the thinker in me rose up and began to question what I was seeing.

What actually took place in what we know as the Holy Land? Was all that I'd learned about God, Jesus, and Holy Spirit true? Am I really standing right in the middle of where it all happened?

Many say, "Seeing is believing." Jesus said to Thomas, one of His disciples, "…because thou hast seen me, thou hast believed: blessed are they that have not seen, and *yet* have believed (John 20:29)." So, I was already at an advantage before journeying to Israel. This was just the icing on the cake.

I walked the streets of the City of David with my own two feet. I walked where Jesus walked and prayed where He prayed. In walking where He walked and praying where He prayed, standing on the ground in Gethsemane was such an experience. I was standing in the place where my Lord prayed with such intensity that blood appeared in His sweat. What intensity! Instead of being stricken solely with joy, I walked away with joy but in conviction. What weighed heavenly on my mind was that I needed to kick my prayer life up a notch. I had to do better if I was going to get the results He got.

Mt. Moriah was next on the agenda. Imagine laying eyes on the mountain where it is said Abraham, after waiting 25 years for his promised child to be born, finally received the promised child Isaac, and then, was instructed to offer him as a sacrifice. We looked upon Mt. Moriah with our own eyes; we walked through the pages of history in person. I touched the point where it is said the cross of Calvary stood. I touched it! I'll admit that I had hoped something miraculous would happen to me, but in my heart of hearts I realize today that my faith was not in action. I was in observation mode.

I saw and touched the stone bed where it is said Mary and the disciples prepared Jesus' body to be laid to rest after His death. I walked inside the tomb where it is said they laid His crucified body to rest. I am happy to report He wasn't there!!!!!!! In an effort not to create any kind of controversy, I made a mental note.

Had the remains of His body been there, the foundation of my faith and countless others would be non-existent.

One of the main points of this tour was the Western Wall. It is believed to be the remains of the great Second Jewish Temple. The Jews consider this area to be sacred ground. On the other hand, many Muslims believe this wall was part of an ancient mosque. Amnon explained that Jews from all over the world as well as many tourists come to this place daily to pray, for it is believed that when you pray here, you have the "ear of God." He pointed out the small pieces of paper lodged in the cracks of the wall and explained that they contain prayers from people all over the world. I asked, "Are we at liberty to leave a prayer?"

As he was indicating that it was OK as long as we did not talk or disturb others as we moved toward the wall, I set my sight on where I was going to place my prayer. Because I'd done a little research ahead of time, I knew the answer would be yes and had come prepared! I had written my prayer the night before....

Hurriedly, I reread and rolled my prayer request into a tiny scroll. After bobbing and weaving my way through the crowd, when opportunity presented itself, I placed my miniature prayer scroll for my family, friends, associates, enemies, and those I was to meet over time in a crack of the Western Wall.

What a feeling! It was a feeling that to this day I cannot fully describe. I wanted to laugh, cry, and sing all at the same time. The least I can say is that the atmosphere appeared to be full of tangible hope. I felt as if my faith expanded, and the love in my heart for mankind thickened. People were hugging and smiling whether or not they knew one another. With all that commotion, it was relatively quiet. The closer I moved toward the Wall, it became quieter as all rendered respect in spite of what one's religious beliefs were. I was fascinated by this and how people governed themselves according to the instructions we'd received. From what I could see, no one needed to call Security.

Standing at the wall, I uttered a simple prayer, "Father, give me the level of wisdom with which you can entrust me." Then, I slowly moved on to allow others the opportunity to make their way to the wall.

Mesmerized by all I'd seen and felt thus far, I was ready to take a break. My spirit was high and lifted up, but my stomach began to raise its own unique sound, the one that lets me know when it is really ready to eat – a growl here and a growl there with less time in between before the next growl made its presence known. The cookies and chips in my snack pack could not satisfy my hunger at this point. I had not eaten breakfast that day and needed food of substance.

Just as the hunger pangs intensified, others in our group began passing the word that we needed to make our way back to our meeting place because it was lunchtime. As I looked around and saw that no one had to be prompted a second time, I chuckled. People were hungry!

The restaurant was a few miles away. Located inside the old city's Jaffa Gate next to the old city wall, the Nafoura Restaurant staff greeted us with the warmest reception. Members of the staff introduced themselves and engaged us all in conversation as they offered us drinks to quench our thirst. They pointed out the patio that runs along the city wall and then led us to the area that was prepared for our group.

Lunch included some good food. If it did not appeal to the stomach, it certainly appealed to the eyes.

They served us a variety of Middle Eastern salads and dip. By this point in the trip, I enjoyed hummus. So, whenever it was available, I ate it. Fish, which was my preferred meat at the time because of health reasons, was served; however, I made my way to the chicken and lamb shish kebab with rice, too. I'm glad I made that choice. The meat was so tender and juicy – it made me wonder why meat in the States didn't taste as good. Was it the seasonings, the chefs, or how the meat was processed that made the difference? As this question formed in my mind, the answer in my mind suggested that Kosher beats processed every time. Even the Coke tasted differently. The variety of fruit tasted ten times sweeter than any fruit I've ever tasted. And, oh! The cookies! Cakes! They were better than delicious.

With bellies full and content, we bid our new restaurant friends adieu and headed back to our drop-off points. For me, that was the Dan Boutique Hotel. I checked in and got the layout of the land if you will. When I got to my room, I paced the floor, still in awe of all that I'd seen on this day. I was so happy and amazed. Above all, I realized just how blessed I was to have the opportunity to touch and see the land of my spiritual heritage. In that moment, it dawned on me that I had not experienced any medical issues – none!

Monday came and the time for me to head for the office had arrived. Just as I was checking out and said my good-byes to the hotel staff, who had been so gracious to me, my driver came in with a sign bearing my name. We connected, exchanged pleasantries, and were on our way. Unlike the other drivers I'd encountered, he obeyed the speed limits.

I spent the entire day meeting and greeting people I'd worked with but had never seen. Finally, it was time to leave for the airport.

I met my driver outside and was really glad he was on time. After talking and smiling all day, my goal was to quietly relax during the ride to the airport. My driver had other plans. I wanted to reflect on my time in Israel; he wanted me to tell him all about my time in Israel. He wanted to know what I thought about this precious land and how being there might have impacted me spiritually.

A Sweet Surprise

We were on our way to the airport. After about ten minutes into the trip, my driver proceeded to pull the car off the road. Needless to say, I was a little uneasy about stopping because there were no stores or anything commercial in sight.

I asked, "Why are we stopping?"

He said, "You'll see." He got out of the car and proceeded to walk out of view. He returned within a minute or two, got back in the car, and said, "This is for you." It was a grapefruit. While I'd seen grapefruit trees in Israel, I'd not eaten a single piece of its fruit.

I admit I was a little reluctant to take it because I'd seen someone pump drugs into a piece of fruit on television, and to add to the paranoia, my dad taught me to never accept things like gum, juicy fruits, or drinks from men that I did not know very well. He told me to never leave my drink unattended when out on a date because the use of date-rape drugs were on the rise. Yes! Dad was very protective.

Nevertheless, my gut instincts told me it was OK to accept and eat the grapefruit. So, I peeled away at it and bit into it with a traditional mindset. *It's just a grapefruit; what's the big deal?* I thought to myself and dare not say what I was thinking out aloud so that I would not offend him in any way.

As I bit into the grapefruit, a burst of the sweetest juice exploded in my mouth. It was like a rain shower of Skittles going on inside my mouth, and with every drop, the sweetness got sweeter. Oh! How succulent it was.

You've never had a grapefruit until you've had one grown in Israel and fresh off the tree, not one that was transported by land, air, or sea.

What a way to end my visit to Israel...yet another new experience, Bible discussions initiated by my driver, and no issues in my body going to Israel, during my stay in Israel, or during my return to the States.

CHAPTER 10

Have No Fear

For six years, I avoided going to see a gastroenterologist, but daily bathed my mind, heart, and thoughts with prayer, praise, and worship. Carefully, I watched the words that came out of my mouth, as well as those I said in my head. I only spoke about what I wanted my outcome to be. By this time in my life, I'd learned what you speak is what you get. Speak negative, you get negative. Speak positive, you get positive. When asked how I was doing, my reply was always, "All is well."

Fast forwarding to the year 2012, something in me nudged me to get a colonoscopy, but I had to find a new doctor. My former gastroenterologist refused to see me any longer because I'd decided not to continue the medication he prescribed.

With this in mind, I called around for gastroenterologists that were in my provider's network. Basically, I took the information of the first doctor they gave me and set up the appointment for the upcoming week. At last, I found a new doctor but did not realize that she just happened to be the partner of the doctor who now refused to treat me.

EAT, PRAY, AND REST

The day of the appointment arrived. I went into the office.

The first thing the doctor said to me was, "You look great! What have you been doing?" That made me smile and feel like a million dollars.

"Eating better, praying, and resting," I replied.

We talked a bit further. I explained my concern about the previous diagnosis and that it was making it hard for me to get insurance. I made it clear that I did not believe I had UC any longer. If that diagnosis had been accurate, the issue was now gone.

She listened very attentively and said, "It's about time to check things out. If things have changed, we'll update the records accordingly, and you should have no more problems getting insurance."

This is what I like about physicians who work *with* patients and listen to their concerns. So, we scheduled a colonoscopy for June 1, 2012.

The day arrived, and I was so happy. "It's a wrap," my faith told me. "What you cannot see with your eyes is already done – you are 'manifestly healed.'" That's the word I heard, which means the thing I'd been praying for and could not see with my natural eyes could now be seen *with* natural eyes.

Thanks to my friend, RB, I did not have to go alone to the appointment. We arrived safely. After checking in, the medical assistant took me to a room to get ready for what was ahead. While waiting, I prayed:

"Holy Spirit, infiltrate my colon with Your presence. For where ever You are, there is fullness of joy. Where You are makes things whole again. Thank You is my prayer."

I fell into a light sleep. An hour or so later, they took me to the testing room where the doctor met me. Knowing I was there for a specific reason, out of the blue, I asked her about the lump on my hand, which I mentioned earlier. She looked and suggested maybe I had hit it against something and bruised it, and we moved on. Yeah, I was trying to get a 2-for-1 checkup. Nonetheless, the anesthesiologist arrived in the interim and was ready to make me happy if you know what I mean. Yes, he was prepared to put me to sleep.

After administering the anesthesia intravenously, he told me to start counting backwards from 100. I challenged him and said I'd make it all the way to zero. He laughed. I started to count, "100, 99…."

You've guessed it. I do not remember getting past 99.

The procedure went very well. My friend came to sit with me until the doctor returned with the report of her findings. Looking at me rather oddly, my doctor approached my bedside.

PICTURE PERFECT

"Don't think I'm strange at what I am about to say," she said. "Your colon is the most beautiful colon I've ever seen. We could use it in the medical books to depict what a healthy colon looks like. I see NO EVIDENCE of UC."

All I could do was exclaim, "I told you! I told you! I told you!"

"Whatever you are doing, you keep on doing it," she said.

"I prayed," I said.

"Well, keep that up! I'll see you in 10 years." she said.

"There were no polyps found in your colon," the final findings stated. "Biopsies were obtained from your colon to rule out a form of colitis."

My friend took me home and made sure I was OK before leaving.

As I sat in my favorite chair, I was watching television and unconsciously rubbing the hand that had the lump on it. I'd developed this habit of rubbing the hand as I prayed about this thing. This time was not the same as it had been. Upon noticing that things felt different, I turned my head and looked down at my hand only to discover the lump was gone!

I got a 2-for-1 deal that day after all - physical proof that bore witness to the healing of my colon and proof that my hand was healed. So, if supernatural healing no longer exists, somebody forgot to give me *that* memo. While I still rely on medical professionals to help manage what may ail my body today, I solely and wholly rely on the One who has proven time and time again, healing is still available to all who will receive.

In the manner that I'd changed my physical diet to help maintain balance in my natural body, I also changed my spiritual diet. I began to more consistently declare God's power over my life and fill my heart and thoughts with the Word of God. Every morning I read the scriptures or listened to them using a Bible app like the YouVersion Bible app. I started my day with prayer, prayed throughout the day, and ended my day with prayer.

I lost all fear of physical death. I did not fear because of this truth. I was fully persuaded that if I died as a result of this disease, my next place of residence would be in the presence of the Lord as stated in 2 Corinthians 5:8: "To be absent from the body is to be present with the Lord." I figured I had nothing to lose if I ended up in His presence. That's the best place to be!

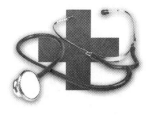

CHAPTER 11

Final Thoughts

Today, I am healed. No more false alarms!

I can eat whatever I want and go wherever I want to go. I still travel a great deal and manage a busy work and ministry schedule. Of course, I consume my guilty pleasures - cookies and chips - in moderation and consult a nutritionist to continue to improve my real diet and overall health. Bottom line? I've decided that I will not help The Enemy cause me to leave Earth prematurely. I monitor what I eat and praise God each time I finish a meal without digestive issues.

All I know is that my Father loves me, and He wants me well. I declared this daily. "No good thing will He withhold from me." That's what the Bible says. That's what I believed.

I am not trying to advise you about seeking medical attention or taking prescription drugs. I only shared my trials and troubles to emphasize how, like Job, and even the Lord, everyone comes to a point of decision. You have to decide whether to place faith in what you know, what someone else knows, or place your life in God's hands. The ultimate goal is to stand on God's promises of wholeness in your mind, body, and soul.

I can tell you that He healed my body. I feel like the Lord spoke to me the way He did the woman who touched the hem of his robe in Mark's gospel, "Daughter, your faith has made you well; go in peace, and be healed of your disease" (Mark 5:34 ESV).

Since those times, other issues have attacked my body.

In one instance, it was to the point of impending death. It was around 8 p.m. one evening in September 2015. I was home alone and had just finished eating dinner. I moved from the dining room to the family room and sat down on the sofa to relax a bit before starting part two of my day – work on this book! About 15 minutes passed by, and suddenly, I felt the urge to clear my throat. Another minute passed, and the urge to clear my throat came again. This was normal in that I frequently dealt with post nasal drip, which results in a tickle in my throat and several attempts to clear.

As I attempted to inhale after clearing my throat a second time, my air passage was blocked. I could not breathe! I raced to the bathroom to see what I could see – nothing. I thought maybe a little water would help. As I attempted to drink some water, the water would not go down. Then I heard a still small Voice say, "Don't panic, and take some Benadryl." Though it would not go down, I took a swig and swished it around in my mouth and the back of my throat. All I could do was squeal and eek out, "Eeeeeeeesus!" That's "Jesus" when you are trying to call His Name, and you cannot breathe. It pays to know you can call upon the Name of the Lord and get the help you need whether or not you are able to call out His Name clearly.

"Call 911," said that same small Voice.

I did, but it was after realizing I was downstairs, and the house and cell phones were upstairs charging. I ran as fast as I could up the stairs and grabbed the house phone. Running back down the stairs, I dialed 911. The 911 emergency dispatcher answered. All I could do was squeal, "I caaaa eeeeth!" That's "I can't breathe" in English, and you literally CANNOT breathe.

Somehow, the lady who took the call understood I was in trouble and immediately dispatched help. Paramedics arrived within 5 to 7 minutes I believe – it was quick. They asked several questions, but I could not speak. When they realized I could not breathe, one of the paramedics gave me a shot of adrenaline that slowly kicked in as they continued to ask questions, put me on the gurney, placed me in the ambulance, and drove me to the hospital. I communicated by nodding my head. Sometimes, I spoke with my hands. And, I used a notepad to write down my replies to the more complex questions they asked.

My throat was totally closed, but somehow I did not blackout and suffered no brain damage. Inconvenienced by a one-night stay in the hospital, I am "thankFULL" that an allergic reaction to "something," which allergy testing failed to identify, didn't take me out. To God be all the glory!

Despite that experience, I continue to stand on God's promises, fight my way through, and reign with victory. I scream inwardly and boldly proclaim as it is written, "O Lord my God, I cried to you for help, and you have healed me...you have brought up my soul from Sheol/hell" (Psalm 30:2 ESV).

We are not the sick trying to get healed. We are the healed. The Enemy tries to convince us that we are sick. I believe that if I open my mind and heart to *receive* what God offers us all in love, I will already *be* healed. I do not have to be sick, nor do you.

A 2016 study by the Barna Group, a source for insights about faith and culture, leadership and vocation, and the generations for more than three decades, shows that most Americans agree.

They report 66 percent of the American adults believe God will heal the body. The third of those surveyed who are skeptics are divided with only about 19 percent in strong disagreement with the idea. A key factor in the willingness to believe seems to be experience.

The study shows Millennials (25 percent) are more than twice as likely to be wary of such faith-based claims as senior citizens (13 percent). The cellphone generation is more in awe of science and technology's power and promises than those manifested through Holy Spirit. Women are more likely to rely on Providence than men. Interestingly, the report shows, "The more education one receives, the less likely they are to believe in supernatural healing."

That is not unusual. The more one acknowledges the need for God, the more they are likely to reach for His help. As a woman with a doctorate and a great career, my belief might seem exceptional. Not really.

The Barna Group study found Evangelicals (87 percent) more likely than any people of faith to buy into the idea that God heals. More than that, Black Americans (55 percent) are the most likely ethnic group to confess such a devout notion. Also, the people who come from the South are most convinced that God can help.

I am a Mississippi-born, black woman, far from being a Millennial in a Bible-based church. I open my mind and heart to Holy Spirit's inspiration. That is why I did not hesitate to plead as the Prophet Jeremiah had done,

"Heal me, O Lord, and I shall be healed; save me, and I shall be saved, for you are my praise" (Jeremiah 17:14). This is why I encourage you.

So, while you wait for the healing to manifest in any part of your being, partner with your medical experts to find an interim solution... unless He tells you otherwise. The point is that we begin to notice how God manifests or reveals Himself every day and include Him in our day-to-day living.

"The manifestation of the Spirit is given to each one for the profit of all," Paul writes in 1 Corinthians 12:7-9. "For to one is given the word of wisdom through the Spirit, to another the word of knowledge through the same Spirit, to another faith by the same Spirit, to another gifts of healings by the same Spirit."

What He did for me, He will do for you because our Father is not a respecter of persons. He is a responder to faith. If supernatural healing no longer exists, I'm sorry. I didn't get THAT memo!

"I pray that you may prosper in all things and be in health, just as your soul prospers," John writes in 3 John 1:2 (ESV). Healing is available to all who will receive it. It may manifest supernaturally, or it may manifest as a result of the assistance of medical professionals. It may be the result of a combination of the two.

Will you believe?

I am the first to admit a walk in faith makes you look strange and crazy. Some might well ask why God does not just heal you without a word, or why He even allows The Enemy to touch you. I cannot fully explain why. To attempt that would result in another book. I can tell you He healed my body.

To step toward that which you and others might not see or understand can make you feel like you are lying to yourself and others. When the doctors told me UC had no known cure, God showed that there is, whether or not they accepted it. When they said I'd have to be on strong medications the rest of my life, I asked the Lord for the protocol for my health. He guided me to find ways to use the Word, food, and exercise as medicine.

Why doesn't God supernaturally heal every sick person?

I cannot fully explain. Perhaps that will be my next book. As stated in the Introduction, this book is to encourage you to include God in the health decision process. This is not a condemnation of the medical profession. I write to assure you that when the wait is over, and the fruit of His promise is clearly delivered, doubters will be in awe.

You *will* have the last say – *Signs and wonders follow those who believe! I believed. Here are my results….*

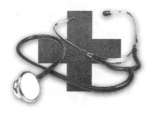

A P P E N D I X   A

The term "heal" and derivatives thereof are mentioned 138 times in the King James Bible as follows: heal (40), healing (14), healed (79), healeth (4), healer (1).

In general, I believe if a topic is mentioned that many times in a single book, it must be a very important one, and there is a message somebody really wants to convey. Here is a list of at least 40 of those times where healing is mentioned or alluded to in the Bible. They help to formulate right thinking when we meditate on them consistently and help us to remain loyal to only speaking what we want our outcome to be in any given situation.

Some of the scriptures listed here are general and give light to the promise of healing to the Israelites based on their obedience; some give an account of healing that took place while Jesus was physically on the earth; the others are direct promises to you and me today – healing is available to all who will receive it. It's a part of the salvation package Jesus offered over 2,000 years ago.

By the way, that offer still stands if you have not received salvation based on John 3:16.

If you want to make that change right now, it's pretty simple. Believe God so loved the world that He gave His only begotten Son. If you believe in Him, you will not perish (remain separated from Him), but you'll have everlasting life.

What is everlasting life? Everlasting life is made up of 2 things.

1. Everlasting life is being reconnected to God through Jesus Christ. It is to know God. To know Him, you must be connected to Him.

2. Everlasting life for you begins the moment you *choose* to accept this as truth, not when you physically die. The connection is completed when you say with your mouth and believe in your heart that God raised Jesus from the dead (Romans 10:9) – at this point, you gain full access to all the provision God has made available to you through the death, burial, and resurrection of His Son, Jesus.

If you just accepted this truth for the first time, welcome to the family of God! Now share the good news with somebody else right now – call them, text them, Face time them – do whatever you need to do to share this experience. Sharing this experience seals the deal.

If you are dealing with any type of disease, keep the Word of God before your eyes. I encourage you to journal your story. And, if it seems that things get worse before they get better, quickly tell the noise of life to shut up! Remember the goal of The Enemy is to kill, still, and destroy.

In the same breath, call on the One who came to give life and life more abundantly – open your mouth, open your heart, and ask Him to help you – it is as simple as saying, "Father, Jesus, or Holy Spirit, help me." Believing you receive the help by faith the moment you pray is the combination that seals this deal! You need both at the same time.

You may not see it with your physical eyes in that moment, but give it the time it needs to manifest. You must participate in activating your healing by watching your words. Words are containers and produce after their own kind. They carry out whatever assignment you put in them. Only speak what you want your outcome to be. Speak negative words; expect an adverse outcome. Speak life; expect life in your outcome. Remember this – the body can do amazing things if the mind and tongue will let it!

Meditate on these healing-based scriptures – it will change your life.

1. If my people, which are called by my name, shall humble themselves, and pray, and seek my face, and turn from their wicked ways; then will I hear from heaven, and will forgive their sin, and will heal their land (2 Chronicles 7:14).

2. O LORD my God, I cried unto thee, and thou hast healed me (Psalm 30:2).

3. Have mercy on me, O LORD; for I am weak: O LORD, heal me; for my bones are vexed (Psalm 6:2).

4. The Lord will strengthen him upon the bed of languishing: thou wilt make all his bed in his sickness (Psalm 41:3).

5. Bless the LORD, O my soul: and all that is within me, bless his holy name. Bless the LORD, O my soul, and forget not all his benefits: Who forgiveth all thine iniquities; who healeth all thy diseases; Who redeemeth thy life from destruction; who crowneth thee with lovingkindness and tender mercies... (Psalm 103:1-4).

6. He sent his word, and healed them, and delivered them from their destructions (Psalms 107:20).

7. He healeth the broken in heart, and bindeth up their wounds (Psalm 147:3).

8. For the LORD God is a sun and shield: the LORD will give grace and glory: no good thing will he withhold from them that walk uprightly (Psalm 84:11).

9. Be not wise in thine own eyes: fear the LORD, and depart from evil. It shall be health to thy navel, and marrow to thy bones (Proverbs 3:7-8).

10. My son, attend to my words; incline thine ear unto my sayings. Let them not depart from thine eyes; keep them in the midst of thine heart. For they are life unto those that find them, and health to all their flesh (Proverbs 4:20-22).

11. But he was wounded for our transgressions; he was bruised for our iniquities: the chastisement of our peace was upon him; and with his stripes we are healed (Isaiah 53:5).

12. Then shall thy light break forth as the morning, and thine health shall spring forth speedily: and thy righteousness shall go before thee; the glory of the LORD shall be thy rereward (Isaiah 58:8).

13. The Spirit of the Lord GOD is upon me; because the LORD hath anointed me to preach good tidings unto the meek; he hath sent me to bind up the brokenhearted, to proclaim liberty to the captives, and the opening of the prison to them that are bound... (Isaiah 61:1).

14. Return, ye backsliding children, and I will heal your backslidings. Behold, we come unto thee; for thou art the LORD our God (Jeremiah 3:22).

15. Heal me, O LORD, and I shall be healed; save me, and I shall be saved: for thou art my praise (Jeremiah 17:14).

16. For I will restore health unto thee, and I will heal thee of thy wounds, saith the LORD; because they called thee an Outcast, saying, This is Zion, whom no man seeketh after (Jeremiah 30:17).

17. Behold, I will bring it health and cure, and I will cure them, and will reveal unto them the abundance of peace and truth (Jeremiah 33:6).

18. Come, and let us return unto the LORD: for he hath torn, and he will heal us; he hath smitten, and he will bind us up (Hosea 6:1).

19. But unto you that fear my name shall the Sun of righteousness arise with healing in his wings; and ye shall go forth, and grow up as calves of the stall (Malachi 4:2).

20. And Jesus went about all Galilee, teaching in their synagogues, and preaching the gospel of the kingdom, and healing all manner of sickness and all manner of disease among the people (Matthew 4:23).

21. And Jesus said unto the centurion, Go thy way; and as thou hast believed, so be it done unto thee. And his servant was healed in the selfsame hour (Matthew 8:13).

22. When the even was come, they brought unto him many that were possessed with devils: and he cast out the spirits with his word, and healed all that were sick... (Matthew 8:16).

23. And Jesus went about all the cities and villages, teaching in their synagogues, and preaching the gospel of the kingdom, and healing every sickness and every disease among the people (Matthew 9:35).

24. And when he had called unto him his twelve disciples, he gave them power against unclean spirits, to cast them out, and to heal all manner of sickness and all manner of disease (Matthew 10:1).

25. Heal the sick, cleanse the lepers, raise the dead, cast out devils: freely ye have received, freely give (Matthew 10:8).

26. Then was brought unto him one possessed with a devil, blind, and dumb: and he healed him, insomuch that the blind and dumb both spake and saw (Matthew 12:22).

27. And Jesus went forth, and saw a great multitude, and was moved with compassion toward them, and he healed their sick (Matthew 14:14).

28. And the whole multitude sought to touch him: for there went virtue out of him, and healed them all (Luke 6:19).

29. And they departed, and went through the towns, preaching the gospel, and healing every where (Luke 9:6).

30. And into whatsoever city ye enter, and they receive you, eat such things as are set before you: And heal the sick that are therein, and say unto them, The kingdom of God is come nigh unto you (Luke 10:8-9).

31. And one of them, when he saw that he was healed, turned back, and with a loud voice glorified God (Luke 17:15).

32. And when Peter saw it, he answered unto the people, Ye men of Israel, why marvel ye at this? or why look ye so earnestly on us, as though by our own power or holiness we had made this man to walk (Acts 3:12)?

33. And now, Lord, behold their threatenings: and grant unto thy servants, that with all boldness they may speak thy word, By stretching forth thine hand to heal; and that signs and wonders may be done by the name of thy holy child Jesus. And when they had prayed, the place was shaken where they were assembled together; and they were all filled with the Holy Ghost, and they spake the word of God with boldness (Acts 4:29-31).

34. To another faith by the same Spirit; to another the gifts of healing by the same Spirit... (1Corinthians 12:9).

35. Is any sick among you? let him call for the elders of the church; and let them pray over him, anointing him with oil in the name of the Lord: And the prayer of faith shall save the sick, and the Lord shall raise him up; and if he have committed sins, they shall be forgiven him (James 5:14-15).

36. Confess your faults one to another, and pray one for another, that ye may be healed. The effectual fervent prayer of a righteous man availeth much (James 5:16).

37. In the midst of the street of it, and on either side of the river, was there the tree of life, which bare twelve manner of fruits, and yielded her fruit every month: and the leaves of the tree were for the healing of the nations (Revelation 22:2).

38. And when the woman saw that she was not hid, she came trembling, and falling down before him, she declared unto him before all the people for what cause she had touched him, and how she was healed immediately (Luke 8:47-48).

39. And he said unto her, Daughter, be of good comfort: thy faith hath made thee whole; go in peace (Luke 8:48).

40. And it came to pass on a certain day, as he was teaching, that there were Pharisees and doctors of the law sitting by, which were come out of every town of Galilee, and Judaea, and Jerusalem: and the power of the Lord was present to heal them (Luke 5:17).

Bonus Scriptures

- And this is the confidence we have in him, that, if we ask any thing according to his will, he heareth us: And if we know that he hears us, whatsoever we ask, we know that we have the petitions that we desired of him (1 John 5:14-15).

- Let us therefore come boldly unto the throne of grace, that we may obtain mercy, and find grace to help in time of need (Hebrews 4:16).

Remember, our Father wants us well, and healing is the children's bread.

Bon áppetit!

A Prayer of Thanksgiving and Healing

Father, we thank You because Your promises are written in eternal ink – they are already kept. As you commanded, *we believe we receive* right now as we pray, and call it as it is – already done. Thank You for Jesus who died *just in case* we would one day decide we wanted to be reconnected to You.

Thank You for healing us before we ever encountered physical, mental, or emotional sickness. Sickness! Disease! Leave our bodies now. We activate through faith the healing that is already ours. You said we were healed, and You cannot lie.

If we were healed, then we are healed. If we are healed, then we shall be healed. We decree and declare that the weapons that form against us will not prosper.

Amen!

Be blessed,
Jackie

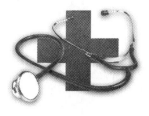

Heart-Letter Bible Verse Memory System

Take Action Now: Review this list of verses and commit them to memory for daily inspiration and to maintain your physical, emotional, mental, and spiritual health. You may want to use this as an exercise to memorize these scriptures on your own, learn with a friend, or if you are a parent or grandparent, learn with your child(ren) or grands.

> And we know that all things work together for good to them that love God, to them who are the called according to his purpose (Romans 8:28).

> But, my God shall supply all your need according to His riches in glory by Christ Jesus (Philippians 4:19).

> Commit thy way unto the Lᴏʀᴅ; trust also in him; and he shall bring it to pass (Psalm 37:5).

> Delight thyself also in the Lord: and he shall give thee the desires of thine heart (Psalm 37:4).

Enter into his gates with thanksgiving, and into his courts with praise: be thankful unto him, and bless his name (Psalm 100:4).

For God so loved the world, that he gave his only begotten Son, that whosoever believeth in him shall not perish, but have everlasting life (John 3:16).

Give, and it shall be given unto you; good measure, pressed down, and shaken together, and running over, shall men give into your bosom. For with the same measure that ye mete withal, it shall be measured to you again (Luke 6:38).

He that hath an ear, let him hear what the Spirit saith unto the churches; To him that overcometh will I give to eat of the tree of life, which is in the midst of the paradise of God (Revelation 2:7).

If my people, which are called by my name, shall humble themselves, and pray, and seek my face, and turn from their wicked ways; then will I hear from heaven, and will forgive their sin, and will heal their land (2 Chronicles 7:14).

*J*esus wept (John 11:35).

*K*nowing this, that the trying of your faith worketh patience (James 1:3).

*L*et not your heart be troubled: ye believe in God, believe also in me (John 14:1).

*M*y soul longeth, yea even fainteth for the courts of the Lord: my heart and my flesh crieth out for the living God (Psalm 84:2).

*N*o weapon that is formed against thee shall prosper; and every tongue that shall rise against thee in judgment thou shalt condemn. This is the heritage of the servants of the Lord, and their righteousness is of me, saith the Lord (Isaiah 54:17).

O give thanks unto the Lord; for he is good; for his mercy endureth forever (1 Chronicles 16:34).

*P*raise ye the Lord. Praise God in his sanctuary: praise him in the firmament of his power (Psalm 150:1).

Quench not the Spirit (1Thessalonians 5:19).

Rejoice in the Lord alway, and again I say, Rejoice (Philippians 4:4).

Study to shew thyself approved unto God, a workman that needeth not to be ashamed, rightly dividing the word of truth (2 Timothy 2:15).

Though wilt keep him in perfect peace, whose mind is stayed on thee: because he trusteth in thee (Isaiah 26:3).

Unto thee Oh! Lord do I lift up my soul. O my God, I trust in thee: let me know be ashamed, let not mine enemies triumph over me (Psalm 25:1-2).

Verily I say unto you, This generation shall not pass, till all these things be fulfilled (Matthew 24:34).

What shall we say then? Shall we continue in sin, that grace may abound? God forbid. How shall we, that are dead to sin, live any longer therein (Romans 6:1-2)?

eXamine me O Lord, and prove me; try my reigns and my heart (Psalm 26:2).

Ye are the light of the world. A city that is set on an hill cannot be hid (Matthew 5:14).

And Zacchaeus stood, and said unto the Lord; Behold, Lord, the half of my goods I give to the poor; and if I have taken anything from any man by false accusation, I restore him fourfold (Luke 19:8).

Heart-Letter Bible Verse Memory Worksheet

Take Action Now: Create your own list of Bible verses and commit them to memory for daily inspiration and to feed your faith.

A. _____
   _____
   _____

B. _____
   _____
   _____

C. _____
   _____
   _____

D. _____
   _____
   _____

E. _____
   _____
   _____

F. _____

G. _____

H. _____

I. _____

J. _____

K. _____

L. _____

M. _____

N. _____

O. _____

_____

_____

P. _____

_____

_____

Q. _____

_____

_____

R. _____

_____

_____

S. _____

_____

_____

T. _____

_____

_____

U. _____

_____

_____

V. _____

_____

_____

W. _____

_____

_____

X. _____
_____
_____

Y. _____
_____
_____

Z. _____
_____
_____

APPENDIX D

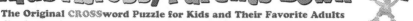

The Original CROSSword Puzzle for Kids and Their Favorite Adults

Share the power of supernatural healing with your child(ren) or grands as you solve the clues based on this book.
The across clues are for kids and the down clues are for grown-ups!

By Jan Buckner Walker

Kids Across

1. It's the time when joy cometh
3. Word blast from the past: In the Bible, it's the past tense of "speak" (Here's a hint: Scramble the letters to find out)
5. Remember, the Bible says that ____ needs work to work (Hint: Take a look at James 2:26)
8. The Lord is (as it says in the title of Chapter 9), "True to ____ Word"
9. Last, but not least: The last book in the Old Testament (It's named after a man whose name means "my messenger")
11. Not in my house!: Jesus evicted (or did this) to unclean spirits (2 words)
14. Ready for a little Bible wordplay?: "Sun of righteousness" is a phrase in Malachi 4:2. Replace one of the words in the phrase with its homonym and see that it will make sense
15. He's the prophet who author Jackie Golden echoed when she pleaded, "Heal me, O Lord, and I shall be healed; save me, and I shall be saved, for you are my praise"
17. The 28th book of the Bible, written by a man whose name means "salvation"
18. God, our Superhero: When the disciples caused the lame man to walk, it made everybody ____ (or the name of a giant comic book company)
19. Each of our spirits ____ in a body (Hint: Check out bullet #2 in Chapter 2)

Parents Down

1. The Fantastic Four: First in sequence (but last in alphabetical order) of the four Gospels
2. Biblically speaking: It's what "nigh" means
3. "He maketh the storm a calm so that the waves thereof are ____" (Psalm 107:29)
4. Prayer is not a "volume" business: As author Jackie Golden notes, "How loudly one prays is not the ____" to answered prayer
6. God did it (and still does!): "He answered their prayers, because they trusted in ____" (1 Chron. 5:20)
7. The City of God mentioned in Jeremiah 30:17
10. Look to the hills: This abbreviation is often found before 7 Down
12. New Testament book of healing: It's not tough to figure out that this follows the four Gospels
13. Number of months in a year or types of fruits in the yield from the Tree of Life
14. Shining and shiny: "For the LORD God is a sun and ____" (Psalm 84:11)
15. Did you know?: This man, who wrote the 59th book of the Bible, was Jesus' half brother
16. Matthew's reminder: "Where your treasure is there your ____ will be also
17. Encouraging word: The Bible mentions this word (including its derivatives) 138 times

Healing Words

119

READERS' COMMENTS

What you are about to read are stories that I have watched unfold in real-life over the past five years. For almost every day during this period, I have engaged in conversations with Jackie. On one occasion, she stared death in the face, and not one time did she accept that it was her time to cross over. The strategies Jackie provides in this book will bless your life.

– **Christopher Coleman** (Clarksdale, Mississippi), Book Project Consultant

Well done thy good and faithful servant! I am speechless, but my mind is at peace. I am encouraged. This is the best read I have seen that helps one to apply the scripture to life. I am healed. No more sickness. No more coughing. I have been awakened to look up and live. Truly, this book is informative and allows the reader to experience many different emotions. I laughed. I cried. I got to know you better, Jackie, and I understand His Word better. I now know how to pray for healing. Thanks for sharing and sending the memo in the form of a book – *Supernatural Healing Exists! Did You Get the Memo?* I got it! God heals in Jesus' Name. I receive it! Keep up the good work, Dr. Jackie!

– **Betty Golphin** (Orlando, Florida), Licensed Psychiatric Social Worker

"He maketh the storm a calm" (Psalms 107: 29 KJV).

The warning that storms will come in everybody's life has been heard since the beginning of time. Some people are frightened. Some become complacent, but thanks be to the almighty God, Jackie accepted the call to pen her storm experiences and expressions. Just as air is a vital source of life, this book contains God's Word that I hope will shed light to the reader of his plan to save human lives. As the warnings of storm arise in your life, *Supernatural Healing Exists...*provides a prolific statement - Come to Jesus now, and receive all that the salvation package offers – healing is just one of many benefits included.

– Ollie Miller (Houston, Texas), Family Friend

The Teacher has hit a home run in presenting Jesus, the Healer, to all who will read this text. Wow! To read about many in the Bible who received supernatural healing is one thing. But, to read about someone who has walked through such an experience in this day and time, achieving results the Bible says we can have, is fascinating and most encouraging. You'll want to read this one and also share it with the ones you love.

– Gwen Ray (Houston, Texas), Executive Coach/Recruiter

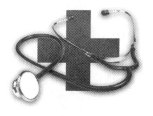

BIBLIOGRAPHY

Barna Group. "The State of the Church 2016 – Research in Faith & Christianity, 2016. https://www.barna.com/research/state-church-2016/.

Bounds, E. M. Praying that Receives Answers. New Kensington: Whitaker House, 1984.

Capps, Charles. The Tongue: A Creative Force. Tulsa: Harrison House, Inc., 1976.

Golden, Jacquelyn D. Dr. Simple Truths: What You Don't Know Can Destroy You – Things I Had to Learn to Start Living. Bloomington: Westbow Press, 2011.

Hagin, Kenneth E. The Believers' Authority. Tulsa: Rhema Bible Church, 1990.

"Ovarian Cancer," last updated 2017. https://www.cdc.gov/cancer/ovarian/index.htm.

"Fibroids," last updated 2017. http://www.misforwomen.com/service/medical-library/conditions/fibroids/.

"The Health Benefits of Tears," updated 2011. http://www.huffingtonpost.com/judith-orloff-md/emotional-wellness_b_653754.html.

"Uterine Fibroids," last updated 2013. https://report.nih.gov/nihfactsheets/ViewFactSheet.aspx?csid=50.

Wigglesworth, Smith. Dare to Believe. Ann Arbor: Servant Publications, 1997.

ABOUT THE AUTHOR

Jacquelyn D. Golden, Ph.D., (a.k.a., Jackie Golden) is an author, motivational speaker, consultant, and entrepreneur who significantly influences the Body of Christ and the marketplace. She promotes the benefits that come with the salvation package that Jesus gave – benefits available for all to freely receive. Often unaware of the instant impact of her words, this sought-after speaker is noted for sharing inspiring, life-changing revelations that flow from her without labor.

Her unique style and delivery leaves a mark of understanding in such a way that those who sit under her teachings are able to recall the content, demonstrations, and life applications years after they receive from her. Because, Jackie makes complex concepts and principles so simple, individuals begin to seamlessly apply the principles in the moment they hear and receive understanding.

Her mission is to change lives one TRUTH at a time.

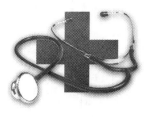

ABOUT THE BOOK

Supernatural Healing Exists!

Did You Get the Memo?

Did supernatural healing end when Jesus ascended back to heaven and returned to His Father? Did supernatural healing cease to exist when Jesus' disciples died? Some will lead you to believe it did.

In this compelling book, author Jacquelyn D. Golden, Ph.D. (a.k.a., Jackie Golden) candidly offers her experience and testimony as tools to help you decide what you will believe about supernatural healing. Hear what she has to say, and discover how she came to her conclusion – supernatural healing still exists!

ENDORSEMENTS

Jackie Golden reminds me of something I know, but am many times "timid" to repeat to non-believers...that God heals. GOD HEALS! Jackie you've given me a precious gift. Not a theological treatise on healing, not an exegesis of scriptures about healing — though there are plenty of wonderful and affirming scriptures to remind us of God's will to heal us. What you've given that's so precious is your own testimony of how God healed **you**. It's one thing to ponder these things when one is well — to hash and rehash the many human opinions on this controversial topic. But when the storm hits, it is a blessing to have Jackie's first-hand testimony of the power of the Almighty to actually heal and restore that which He has created.

Kirk Whalum, Saxophonist/Composer

Long before Jacquelyn's earthly birth, this "Golden Girl" was chosen by God to be uniquely blessed, broken, healed, and delivered. This faith-building book should inspire any reader to deeper spiritual consciousness and gratitude. Dr. Golden's extraordinary personal testimonials are viscerally riveting. Therefore, assuredly, on anyone's life journey, through every challenge, the Highest Source of Divine Power can permeate all debilitating crises and one's soul can soar and take the wings of faith, hope, and love. Glory to God!!!

Sara Jordan Powell/Ministries
Fourth Generation Member
Church of God in Christ, Inc.
Oklahoma Northwest Jurisdiction
Tulsa, Oklahoma

Supernatural Healing Exists! Did You Get the Memo? by Dr. Jacquelyn D. Golden is an inspirational and valuable treasure for anyone encountering the dreadful agony of sickness and disease. With strong faith and a champion-styled heart, Dr. Golden chronicles her personal journey through medical fears and terrifying illness, and masterfully concludes that supernatural healing is a modern reality that anyone can experience and enjoy. Indeed, her profound memoir serves as a sweet memorandum to all that Almighty God still heals! Each chapter pulsates with divine truth and shines a scriptural light in the midst of darkness. With documented joy, this timeless narrative celebrates life-giving possibilities and renews great hope in the faint of heart. I highly recommend its testifying pages to all in search of miraculous healing and spiritual restoration.

Dr. Yolanda Powell

Minister, Author & Speaker

Yolanda Powell Transcontinental, LLC

Upper Marlboro, Maryland USA

Printed in the United States
By Bookmasters